Women, Faith, and Economic Justice

Edited by Jackie M. Smith

In cooperation with the
Justice for Women Working Group
Division of Church and Society
National Council of the Churches of Christ
in the U.S.A.

The Westminster Press
Philadelphia

Unless otherwise identified, Scripture quotations are from the Revised Standard Version of the Bible, copyrighted 1946, 1952, © 1971, 1973 by the Division of Christian Education of the National Council of the Churches of Christ in the U.S.A., and are used by permission.

ISBN 0-664-24600-1

Book design by Gene Harris

First edition

Published by The Westminster Press®
Philadelphia, Pennsylvania

PRINTED IN THE UNITED STATES OF AMERICA

9 8 7 6 5 4 3 2 1

For Susan, Jason, and Oliver
who for me personalize future generations,
creativity, and hope

God has arranged all things in the world
in consideration of everything else.

As often as the elements,
the elements of the world
are violated
by ill-treatment,
so God will cleanse them.

God will cleanse them
thru the sufferings,
thru the hardships
of humankind.

Now in the people
that were meant to green,
there is no more life of any kind.
There is only shrivelled barrenness.

The winds are burdened
by the utterly awful stink of evil,
selfish goings-on.

Thunderstorms menace.

The air belches out
the filthy uncleanliness of the peoples.

There pours forth an unnatural,
a loathsome darkness,
that withers the green,
and wizens the fruit
that was to serve as food for the people.

Sometimes this layer of air
is full,
full of a fog that is the source
of many destructive and barren creatures,
that destroy and damage the earth,
rendering it incapable
of sustaining humanity.

The first seed of the longing for Justice
blows through the soul like the wind.

The taste for good will plays in it
like a breeze.

The consummation of this seed
is a greening in the soul
that is like that
of the ripening world.

Now the soul honors God
by the doing of just deeds.

The soul is only as strong as its works.

—Hildegard of Bingen, 1098–1179

CONTENTS

Grateful acknowledgment for permission to reprint material is made to the following:

American Council of Life Insurance, for information used to prepare the Fact Sheet on Women and Work, pages 24-25. Community and Consumer Relations, American Council of Life Insurance, 1850 K Street NW, Washington, DC 20006.

American Friends Service Committee, for the story of Min Chong Suk, pages 13-15, excerpted from the pamphlet *The Market of Human Beings,* published in English in 1978.

Bear & Company, for the epigraph on page 2 from *Meditations With ™Hildegard of Bingen* by Gabrielle Uhlein. Permission granted by Bear and Company, Inc., PO Drawer 2860, Santa Fe, NM 87504.

Christianity and Crisis, for "Working Women and the Male Workday" by Rosemary Ruether, on pages 53-56. Reprinted with permission. Copyright © 1977, Christianity and Crisis, Inc., 537 West 121st Street, New York, NY 10027.

Fellowship of Reconciliation, Box 271, Nyack, NY 10960, for the World Peace Prayer on page 42.

Global Education Associates, for material on pages 26 and 38 by Patricia M. Mische, from "Women, Power, and Alternative Futures," *The Whole Earth Papers,* No. 8, Part I, Global Education Associates.

The Rev. Barbara A. Greene-Hurd, founder with Nancy Lyman of the Survivors' Network, for excerpts used in Alternatives to Crisis Living, pages 52-53.

Institute for New Communications, for "Around the World with Multinational Corporations," pages 16-20, from *Women in the Global Factory* by Annette Fuentes and Barbara Ehrenreich, © Institute for New Communications, distributed by South End Press, 302 Columbus Avenue, Boston, MA 02116, pp. 5-15, 25-26, 34-35, 41-42, 55-57.

Mother Jones magazine, for excerpts from "The Left's Best Hope" by Barbara Ehrenreich and Frances Fox Piven used in the discussion of the feminization of poverty on pages 48-49, and for "A New Kind of Office Politics" by Dan Marschall, pages 56-58.

Network, A Catholic Social Justice Lobby, 806 Rhode Island Avenue NE, Washington DC 20018 (202-526-4070), for material from their newsletters used on pages 50-51.

Newspaper Enterprise Association, for the Berry's World cartoon on page 15.

Pantheon Books, a division of Random House, and Hodder & Stoughton Ltd., for the stories of Gaynell Begley and Ramona Bennett (pages 10-12 and 21-23), from *American Dreams: Lost and Found* by Studs Terkel. Copyright © 1980 by Studs Terkel. Reprinted by permission. Also, Norma Millay Ellis, for six lines quoted by Gaynell Begley from the poem "Renascence," from *Collected Poems,* published by Harper & Row, copyright 1917, 1945 by Edna St. Vincent Millay.

Praeger Publishers, for the story of Lucia on page 15, from *Making It Happen: A Positive Guide to the Future,* a project of the U.S. Association for the Club of Rome, ed. by John M. Richardson, Jr.

Presbyterian Church (U.S.A.), for "God Does and Demands Justice" (page 32), from the 196th (1984) General Assembly's statement on "The Christian Faith and Economic Justice," and for "Work Sheet for Creating a New Society" (page 45), from study materials prepared for this statement.

Roundtable Press, for quotations on page 21 from *Green Paradise Lost* by Elizabeth Dodson Gray. Copyright © 1979 by Elizabeth Dodson Gray. Permission by Roundtable Press.

SANE—Committee for a Sane Nuclear Policy, 711 G Street SE, Washington, DC 20003—for "Do You Know What Your Tax Dollar Buys?" (page 41) from the flyer of the same name; the flyer "Guide to the Military Budget FY '85" was used in preparing pages 36-37.

SELFHELP Crafts, 240 North Reading Road, Ephrata, PA 17522, for the quotation from their brochure "What is SELFHELP Crafts?" on page 53 titled "One Woman's Initiative."

Socialist Review, for excerpts from the article "Women and the State: Ideology, Power and the Welfare State" by Frances Fox Piven, quoted on page 50, from *Socialist Review #74* (March-April 1984).

Theology in the Americas, 475 Riverside Drive, New York, NY 10115, for Economic Consciousness Razors on page 23, adapted from The Women's Project, Theology in the Americas.

The Washington Post, for the chart "The Arms Race" on page 36 and for quotations from the article "Thinking the Unthinkable" by Rick Atkinson on page 37.

The Witness, Episcopal Church Publishing Company, and Sheila Collins for portions of the article "Reclaiming the Bible Through Storytelling" on pages 30-32, from Document No. 3 of a series distributed by the Secretariat of Theology in the Americas in New York, resulting from work with the TIA Women's Project "Women, Work, and the Economy." The article first appeared in *The Witness* magazine, September 1978.

Women's International League for Peace and Freedom, 1213 Race Street, Philadelphia, PA 19107, for "Balancing the Budget on the Backs of Women," pages 39-40.

INTRODUCTION

A Challenge to Women

The purpose of this workbook is to help women learn more about women and economics; about the planet we share with men, who in the past have been our primary economic decision makers; and about our future, especially the need for women to help shape new, just, fulfilling, and ecologically sound economic structures.

Often in the past our Christian heritage has fostered a negative, almost hands-off attitude toward economic structures, because they deal with material needs and goods. Yes, the biblical message does indicate that wealth and riches cannot bring true happiness. Certainly the life eternal revealed through Jesus Christ is more than can be promised by any economic system. And yet Jesus opened his ministry preaching "good news to the poor . . . release to the captives . . . sight to the blind . . . and liberty [to] those who are oppressed" (Luke 4:18). Let us also reflect on John 3:16–17: "For God so loved the *world* that [God sent the] only Son, that whoever believes in him should not perish but have eternal life. For God sent the Son into the world, not to condemn the world, but that the *world* might be saved through him" (emphasis added). This affirmation refers not simply to the individual but, rather, to God's saving act for the *kosmos,* or *oikoumene,* the whole inhabited earth in God, the one world.

As Larry L. Rasmussen tells us (p. 18),*

Oikoumene is a Greek word, from *oikos,* or "house." Economics, ecumenical, and ecology are all words that share this same root. The One World is the house. *Economics* means providing for the household's needs and managing it well. *Ecumenical* means seeing the inhabitants as a single family and fostering the family's unity. *Ecology* refers to the knowledge of that interdependence upon which the very life of the house depends."

Within the broader framework of God's saving work of the *oikoumene,* we see the crucial importance of economics for those who follow

_____
* The complete reference for this quotation, and others similarly cited, appears under Further Reading at the back of the book.

Christ. Julius K. Nyerere remarked, "To the starving, good and assured food is the quality of life. For a woman who now has to walk miles for water, a village tap might mean life itself." What quality of life is there for the quarter of the world's families who live in absolute poverty or the additional half who are the poor? For that matter, what quality of life is possible for those of us in the remaining quarter, who live in material abundance with the knowledge that millions of the world family, mostly children, die each year from malnutrition and related causes? To intensify the situation, there is a growing disparity between the rich and the poor, the exploited and the exploiters, the powerful and the powerless. This condition leads to systems and life-styles that diminish and corrupt the potential for fullness of life for rich and poor alike.

The crises that face us are not only in economic relationships but also in ecological and ecumenical relationships. The deterioration of these relationships within the whole inhabited world creates a fear-filled, negative, and foreboding picture, not only of the present but also of the future. Such realities easily make us feel powerless and doomed. For this reason we must remember that every crisis has a positive side.

Any crisis is a turning point that offers the possibility of radical change, positive change as well as negative change. As in the crisis of an illness, when a turning point occurs leading to recovery or death, so a historical crisis presents us not only with a fearful view of doomsday but also with extraordinary challenge and hope. Although a crisis is a time of imminent danger, it also contains the possibility of new and more humane, creative, and life-giving social arrangements.

Our images of reality and our visions of the future determine our priorities. As we see our future, so we act. As we act, so we become. We can bring about desirable changes when we see new directions and act to achieve them.
—"At the Crossroads," p. 3

Helvi Sipila, who was appointed in 1972 as Assistant Secretary-General for Social Development and Humanitarian Affairs of the United Nations, emphasized how critical is women's participation in creating new visions of the future that can change our priorities in the present:

> Which is the new force necessary to create a new faith and confidence among people and nations, and to direct the human and material resources into constructive purposes, instead of destructive? Who are those who have not participated in building the present situation? If there is any such group, the largest must be the women of the world. They could become the new, dynamic force to create change, change in the minds, attitudes, behavior, and action of all people.

Can Women Become Agents for Change?

The Second International Women's International League for Peace and Freedom Congress, held in Zurich in 1919, stated:

> An equal moral standard between men and women should be recognized. . . . Women should have the same pay as men for the same work. All professions, trades, and industries should be open to women, and the training for these should be available to men and women alike. Women should have the same opportunities for education, including technical education, as men and the opportunity to enter trade unions on the same terms. . . . Work in connection with the home and family, as well as industrial work, should be organized in such a way that women may make their fullest . . . contribution to the community.

This dream has never been realized. Indeed, present unjust economic arrangements and the political, social, and military systems that sustain them challenge both men and women to seek patterns for more humane and just relationships on both the local and global scale. Yet most women historically have turned their energies to providing relief for the economic system's victims. Although relief must be given, relief alone actually helps to keep unjust structures alive and healthy, thereby producing additional persons who suffer from oppression. Most likely, these will be women.

Churchwomen particularly have been caught in a bind: They are especially sensitive to issues of justice relating to others and see these needs as more important than their own needs, acknowledged or unacknowledged. At the same time, these women have failed to see the relation between their own oppression and sense of powerlessness and the multiple crises on the national and international economic scene. It is imperative to place our study of economics and work within the larger picture of global inter-connectedness. In this broader framework, we can identify all the forces that impinge on our own economic issues. For example: Women's struggle for equal opportunity, access, and wages in the growth-oriented economy of the United States must be viewed within the context of an age of scarcity that forces us to recognize the finite limitations of the earth's resources. This view raises new questions about the nature and meaning of work—indeed, about life itself—and about power, control, and decisions about the distribution of resources that affect the lives of all people in our global community.

When the larger economic picture is considered, it becomes difficult for women in the United States—particularly those viewing the problem from a perspective of Christian faith—simply to seek a fairer share of the pie, be it a power or a resource pie. Rather, we must become involved in a struggle to create a quite different pie if anyone in our world is to be liberated. We cannot claim for ourselves the same dehumanizing, alienating, exploitative modes of work that characterize our present economic arrangements. Rather, if our world is to survive, women who are concerned for more fulfilling work and greater economic justice in this country must also discover vital connections with the struggle for justice and liberation of other exploited and oppressed groups, nations, and peoples. As we begin to trace the web of crucial connections between the converging crises in sexism, racism, economic exploitation, escalating violence, militarism, and the technological control and depletion of our earth, we will bring into sharper focus the common origin of all major global crises: a pattern of domination and subordination for structuring life.

Affluent women who analyze this root cause of interdependent crises can see that their oppression as women is caused by the same kinds of systems that oppress Third World persons. Their struggle for liberation is not just for themselves; it is necessary for the survival of the world. The same is true for women of the Third World. The struggle is one. For both groups, an essential part of "their" struggle is "our" struggle and vice versa. The visions, hopes, and dreams that shape our economic activities, struggles, and longings must reflect the truth that liberation in the sphere of work and economics must begin to come communally for the whole human family or not at all. A revolution in economic practices and systems is already taking place in our time. We are experiencing God's judgment upon economic arrangements that exploit not only people and nations but also the earth. Such a situation raises some key questions.

1. What will it mean for women to put on the prophet's cloak and point not only to God's act of judgment but also to God's will for new, life-giving, alternative ways of arranging economic life?

2. How can women, an economically oppressed and exploited group, still striving for full access to political and economic systems, hope to become a powerful force to bring about the kind of revolutionary changes needed?

3. How can women avoid being assimilated into the "manmade" system of economic domination which makes their own and other people's oppression not only possible but necessary?

In this complex and difficult area there are no easy answers, but there are indications of the directions in which women need to move.

First, women need to develop a new consciousness, which perceives the hidden possibilities in human life for more just and fulfilling economic arrangements that will meet real (not created) human need, preserve the earth, and create conditions for richer human interaction. Who more than women are in touch with what is really needed to create, nurture, and sustain human life? Who is more in tune with natural life processes, both organic and inorganic? Women's major energies should not be directed toward trying to reform an economic system that is already reaping the consequences of its self-destructive roots. Rather, women are needed to give birth to the new.

Second, women need to lift up those values and life processes that can transform economic relationships. The values and behaviors traditionally labeled "feminine"—love, cooperation, receptivity, patience, compassion, and a strong sense of justice—are essential to the development of economic systems that place primary value on life-sustaining and creative activities, as contrasted with the dominance, control, mastery, competition, and consumption values of the present system.

Third, women need to be challenged to begin and to continue the difficult process of liberating themselves from exploitative economic systems and practices. In doing so, they not only will provide alternative visions for themselves and others but also will provide the resources for experimenting with new ways of arranging economic relationships.

About This Workbook

This is not an ordinary workbook. It will raise questions, issues, and concerns that cannot be answered simply by referring to information contained here. This workbook is not meant to give you all the answers or sell you on a particular theory of economics. The information and exercises it provides will encourage you to sharpen your critical appraisal of our government's policies, especially as they relate to economics and the military. Since we have primary responsibility for those policies, and because it is in our nation that we have the power to bring about change, we must examine our own country most closely. Of course, because of the United States' position of power in the world, change here will facilitate change elsewhere.

This workbook is created to involve you in a discovery process through which you can do the following:

1. Uncover information you already have available to you through analysis of the effects of today's economic arrangements on your family, your own growth and development, your education and work, your values and goals, and your religious beliefs.

2. Begin to trace the impact of economic realities on the lives of others in the global family.

3. Explore what the Bible has to say about the relationship of faith and economics.

4. Begin to envision alternative ways of arranging economic life that could more nearly reflect biblical concerns and values.

5. Decide for yourself what basic changes are needed if we are to create more humane and just economic relationships.

6. Commit yourself to a course of action to work for change.

Tools You Will Need

It is assumed that each person who uses the workbook will have a Bible. Newspapers and general and women's magazines can be obtained in your local library if you don't subscribe to them. There is also a section of resources and a reading list in the back that will help you find additional information as you need it.

If you are not using the workbook with a group, you might want to ask a few people to study with you. Since your background provides you with only one person's experience and perceptions, it would be especially helpful to select people from diverse racial, ethnic, national, or class origins. A leader's guide written for group use of this workbook is provided in the back. It contains suggestions about people you might consider as possibilities for study with you.

If you cannot join with others, you will find help in the stories of women from different backgrounds contained in the text. These stories will help you gather data about the impact of economics on women from a wide spectrum of life, as will the many interviews to be found in Studs Terkel's *Working* and *American Dreams: Lost and Found,* collections that communicate not only the interviewees' experiences but also their innermost fears, hopes, and dreams. Perdita Huston's *Third World Women Speak Out* is also helpful. These books and many others are listed at the back.

PART ONE

Economics, Past and Present

SECTION 1

Beginnings

The exercises in this first section are designed to help you get in touch with the way work and economic arrangements influence human life, especially the lives of women.

Reflections on Where to Begin

Economics is an extremely complex and confusing subject. In the past, a majority of people have simply accepted (or complained about) the realities of existing economic structures. Change or defense of the status quo has by and large been left up to government economists—the experts. Today, all of us must consider the impact of our collective economic life on personal, national, and international levels. Here are the reasons:

1. Control and distribution of material resources (always linked with power) are prime factors in national and international oppression, violence, militarism, and nuclear threat.
2. The world hunger problem continues to threaten our global family, with between 13 and 19 million persons dying of starvation yearly.
3. Economic realities continue to be a major influence in political and military decisions, both in the United States and in the world at large.
4. Economic life of necessity affects not only the body but also the personal and spiritual life, in many direct and indirect ways.
5. Economic life is a central focus of the Christian faith, for an estimated 80 percent of Jesus' teachings deal with mammon and its effects on individual and communal life.

To begin your reflection, try honestly to face where you are with economics by completing the two sentences below:

1. When I think of economics, I —————.
2. In my mind, faith and economics mix like —————.

Entering Into the Stories of Others

A primary source for learning about the impact of economic life on the individual and on community life is hearing about the experiences of other people and analyzing the effects on their lives. Gaynell Begley's statement is from Studs Terkel's *American Dreams: Lost and Found.* Gaynell and her husband, Joe, own a small general store in Blackey, Kentucky, in the Cumberland Mountains. Her experiences, which reflect those of many mountain people in the United States, put us in contact with what happened to ordinary people as the control of natural resources became concentrated in the hands of the few and, later, as the U.S. economy shifted from coal to oil as a major energy source. Gaynell's intimate reflections illuminate how economic arrangements in the United States affect personal lives in particular and human affairs in general. As you read her story, note the economic forces impinging on the community of Blackey.

Gaynell Begley

Forty-five years ago [says Joe], Blackey was an incorporated town. There were seven coal mines here, deep minin'. They had six passenger trains here a day. We had a bank, we had a drugstore, we had an ice plant, we had a hotel, we had two or three restaurants. Along about 1927, they had a tremendous flood here that destroyed a lot of things. Immediately after that, the depression wiped some more out. It's been a battle ever since.

To me, the mountains here has been kind of a wild animal refuge for people. I don't think people know the history of Appalachia. . . .

[Gaynell] is behind the counter at the store. There is a steady stream of customers: small children, old people, husky young men off the road repair gang. The sales: a Coke, a bag of potato chips, a carton of milk, a loaf of bread. No Rolls-Royce salesman is any more solicitous of his patrons. She addresses each by name. There are constant soft, jocular exchanges. "A transaction here is not entirely economic. It's a matter of friendship and socializin' for a minute. That's as important to me as gettin' that quarter."

This is America to an awful lot of people who don't really realize it's bein' pulled out from under 'em. That's the only time I get scared. I'm not really pessimistic at all, but I do hate to see certain things go. I got a letter from my sister who lives in Eddyville, but it's got a Paducah postmark. It's such a small thing, but it just tears me up. It's typical of the thinkin' of big government. What does the Eddyville postmark mean to them? Or Blackey?

It's not the same kind of population I grew up with. Just about every house then had father, mother, and a group of children. Now about every third house is a widow whose children have gone to Ohio or Michigan to get a job. Most of 'em would like to come back if they could make a livin'. Our elementary school in Blackey covers the first eight grades. Seventy percent of the hundred twenty students are eligible for free lunches. That tells you somethin' about the town. It's just heartbreakin'.

We have a lot of sick people. The men who've worked so long in the mines have black lung or—this man who was just in here without hands. They were blown off in a dynamite cap accident. There's not the same spirit in the town. Well, of course, there's not the same spirit in me. My mother and daddy had a restaurant. We're talkin' about the middle twenties, before the crash. She made all the pies herself, oh Lord, the most fantastic pies. It was a real busy place. The coal mines were workin'. Then, it was the expectancy. Things were going to happen to me in the future. Now it's just an awful lot of lookin' backward.

I'm ashamed of my expectations because now I know a lotta things I didn't know then. Advice from older people I respected was: Hurry up, get educated, and get out. I really didn't do any deep thinkin' about myself, who I was, what I could be. I just didn't think I'd ever come back to eastern Kentucky. I marked it off my list. (Laughs.)

I went to Berea College and then to New England to work. I had no idea that to be a moutaineer, to be an Appalachian, to be a hillbilly, was somethin' a person would be remotely proud of. I was terribly ashamed of it and didn't want anybody to know when I left here. In Connecticut, '39 and '40, I would try to talk the way they talked to show everybody I'd risen above bein' a hillbilly. I'm well over it now. Joe took care of that. (Laughs.)

Oh, I was really proud of my family. But back in my head, I'd keep thinkin': Why did such fine people stay in such a place? They could have gone to the bluegrass country. I really would not like to have been a mountaineer. Then I met Joe and, boy, there was nothin' about him that he was ashamed of. That was really great.

My daddy's name, Caudill, is one of the commonest around here. That's 'cause they were early settlers, dating back to the American Revolution. George Washington paid off some of his soldiers with land grants instead of money. One of his young soldiers was a James Caudill from North Carolina. For his payment he received several hundred acres. This was called Virginia at the time. He came here just before the 1800s and settled about two miles up. He was my grand-

father's grandfather, unless I've left off a "great" somewhere. (Laughs.) Oh yes, we've been here a long time.

The idea that our land was no longer ours first came to me when I was about sixteen or seventeen. I was wantin' desperately to go to college, but there was absolutely no money. Yet down the road was a girl who was gettin' ready to go to college, with trunks and trunks of clothes. Her parents owned the mine. But it was my grandpa's land. Somewhere in my mind was the idea that there was somethin' at odds here. You can't believe how many years it took me to get to the root of the problem: the broad-form deed. This absentee owner is the same as the few men who own America, really.

What really makes me mad is when people talk about the poor. I'm not real sure who they are talkin' about. To me, the people who come in here happen to be desperately poor. But they're Stella and Uncle Wash and Bob. They're individuals. Bein' poor is just one more part of 'em as people. I wish they weren't. But they're not somebody on paper, just a percentage to us.

My daddy was a really, really patriotic person. He so strongly believed that the government was good and the government will protect you. I once believed that, but I no longer do. I'm not patriotic the same way my daddy was. I don't have this terribly nationalistic feelin' at all. I just can't see the insanity of dividin' the world into countries. Not that I want everything to blend. I love the diversity: the different look and the different speech and the different people. But I just feel one-worldish. (Laughs.)

What is education? I don't know how you get it. I think when you're educated, you're able to view things realistically and see yourself as part of a community and that community as part of the world. There's somethin' inside you that propels you. It's not without, with an educated person. If he's answerable to himself, he's an educated man.

When I was a little girl, I loved to read. One of the series of books my mother bought me was *The Chinese Twins*. There were *The English Twins*, *The Scottish Twins*, a series of books. They were really real to me. Here were these children from all over the world, but they weren't all that different from me. That's the earliest I can remember of people bein' different but still all part of the family.

I like poetry awful well, and Edna St. Vincent Millay wrote one when she was about eighteen. She said:

All I could see from where I stood
Was three long mountains and a wood;
I turned and looked another way,
And saw three islands in a bay.

And then it goes on to say—oh, darn. (Laughs.)

11

A man was starving in Capri;
He moved his eyes and looked at me.

You know, she saw over the hills to the rest of the world. It just touched me early, early, early, and made me think I was kin.

Questions for Reflection

1. What happened to the people of Blackey?
2. What changes might occur in economic life if more people felt as "one-worldish" as Gaynell does?
3. Referring to Millay's poem, what value can you find in turning and looking the other way?

Getting in Touch with Your Past

Taking a trip into your past will help you identify some economic factors that have been formative in your life. Read the listed directions two or three times, and then close your eyes and let your body relax. A helpful technique for centering and relaxing is paying attention to your breathing. Take a big breath and, as you exhale, say the word *relax*. Do this several times until you feel tension flowing out of your body with each exhalation. Then, pretending you have a movie projector and film, project the following on your mental screen as you move slowly through your memory trip:

The child you were at about ten years of age
The town, city, or countryside where you lived
The kind of people you grew up with
The major ways people made a living where you lived
The dwelling where you lived at age ten (walk in and look around)
Now watch yourself at play: What are you doing, and with whom?
What are you wearing? How do you feel about yourself?
What did you want to be when you grew up?
What dreams did family members have for your future?

Jot down any new insights you have uncovered about economic forces in your family or community.

Writing Your Economic History

In order to understand more fully how economics affects your life, write your past economic history. Start your story as far back as you have knowledge and move to the present. Use the following questions (adapted from Harry Strharsky, ed., *Must We Choose Sides?*) as well as Gaynell's story as a guide to the sorts of things to include.

1. What did your great-grandparents, grandparents, mother, and father do for a living? Who were the primary wage earners in each household? Who were the primary decision makers about how money was spent and about other major decisions, such as where the family lived?
2. How did these people feel about their work? How did others perceive their work? If your mother did not have a job outside the home, how, at age ten, would you have answered the question, Does your mother work? If she did, how did you and your family value her job? Did you feel differently about your father's work? If so, how and why?
3. What factors motivated or conditioned their particular work? If certain economic or educational circumstances had been different, would they have chosen other vocations?
4. What factors caused them either to make or not make major changes in their lives (such as moving to a different geographical location, getting married, having children, getting further education)? Try to relate these changes to shifts that were occurring in the economy or to major sociopolitical events at that time.
5. How do you think your family's economic (class) background affected you? How do you think your parents' understanding of "women's work" affected you? How have both affected your self-image, your work expectations, your education, your feelings about your parents, and your perceptions of others? How have your education and work influenced the kind of person you now are: your values, perceptions, beliefs, hopes and dreams, the way you relate to others and yourself?
6. What was your earliest contact with some person(s) who was poor? Rich?
7. What religious themes stand out in your story? How is your religious belief and practice influenced by your economic background and present experience?

After completing your economic history, answer these questions:

1. What similarities or differences did you find in your story and Gaynell's?
2. What relationship did you find between racism, sexism, and economics?
3. In what ways do economic realities affect family members' growth and development, their perceptions, expectations, values, attitudes, and beliefs?
4. What else did you learn?

SECTION 2

How Women's Lives Are Shaped by Work and Economic Realities

The material included in this section is intended to put you in touch with, first, the way work and economic arrangements influence the lives of Third World women from diverse ethnic, cultural, racial, and national backgrounds, and, second, the role work activities play in shaping these women's values and beliefs about themselves, other people, the world, and ultimately God.

Reflections on a Choice

Many of our sisters around the world are faced with life situations created by economic realities some of us cannot even imagine. As you read this poem, try to stand in your sister's place.

The Arithmetic of Poverty
Decide, mother,
who goes without.
Is it Rama, the strongest,
or Baca, the weakest
who may not need it much longer,
or perhaps Sita?
Who may be expendable.
Decide, mother,
kill a part
of yourself
as you resolve the dilemma,
Decide, mother,
decide. . . .
   APPADURA (India)
   Quoted in Richardson, p. 113

Entering Into the Stories of Others

Although the two stories that follow are intended to help us feel and think with our sisters in other countries, it is also true that similar stories are being lived daily by women in Appalachia, in the Sun Belt, in the "new" sweatshops of New York, Boston, and Los Angeles, in textile and electronic factories in North Carolina, in migrant tents and barracks, by refugees and immigrants throughout the United States. As you read the stories, try to stand in the shoes of each, to see and think and feel from their viewpoint. It would be especially helpful to underline all the questions raised by Min Chong Suk.

Min Chong Suk

Min Chong Suk operates a sewing machine in Seoul, Korea's, Peace Market Garment District. She is one of approximately 300,000 textile workers who have contributed to South Korea's "economic miracle" but have seen little of its fruits.

My day starts with my mother's voice waking me—"Get up! It's already 6:30"—oh, I have to get up. I shouldn't spoil myself. But six hours' sleep is too short for me. I leave my home at 7 A.M., come back around 11:30 P.M., and take a supper around midnight. This is my schedule every day.

Our room is not so small since it measures nine meters square, but one part is used for the kitchen and another part for drawers and a desk. There's not enough space for the seven members of our family to sleep. I have difficulty finding my place to sleep when I get back at midnight even if my mother asks my younger brothers to leave a place for me.

Seven o'clock is still somewhat dark. Walking through the barracks I can hear the noise of plates clapping which sounds so sad to me. Most of the people here live like me. They go to work early in the morning and get back late at night. Rush hour for this community's bus is seven to eight in the morning and ten to eleven in the evening. We work longer hours than regular persons, twice as long as them. Why are we now so poor and never able to escape?

We have a strong will to have a better life. Why is our life getting worse day by day? Something must be crazy. . . .

All of the passengers on the bus are young girls around twenty years old, except for the students. We all have the same hard life. We are bound together with one string and are exploited and restrained. Why can't we cut this dirty string? I have no idea. When people resisted in Chong Kye chon several years ago against the government policy which evicted us from our houses there, bulldozers came and took down our barracks in a minute. Poor people should be united, but how? If we were united, could we make any change—with the many rich people and government officials with their money and their rights?

After a one-hour ride, the bus arrives at the factory. It looks like a jail—a brick building with only a few windows. Our working room is a big hall divided into several sections by thin wooden partitions. On the hall side there are no windows. Maybe the company doesn't want people to be able to look in. It smells of dust. Several ventilators are not enough for this large messy room with materials, sewing machines, and people.

The wage system has many amazing points here: Legally the *shidas* (young female apprentices) should receive a monthly salary from the managers or be paid by the hours they actually worked. But the managers pay such a small amount that the sewing machine operators feel sorry and help the shidas. This means the shidas must be dependent on both the managers and the operators. They devote their bodies, hearts, growth, and everything for that 8,000 won a month.

After paying transportation fees, the shidas have only enough money left for one bowl of buckwheat soup. It's amazing that their small earnings are the largest income for their families. Heran's father has left home. Her mother used to sell fish on the street to make a living, but when the road was relocated as part of the "Saemaul" movement, she lost her job. Now she earns 200–300 won per day by making envelopes at home. Other shidas' lives are similar to Heran's in this Peace Market. When I asked Heran what she wants to be in the future, she answered, "I want to be a good sewing machine operator like you."

Heran said she wanted to be a skillful sewing machine operator like me. I can understand her hope, since I had the same at her age. You don't know if you don't become an operator. We have so many diseases—bronchitis, indigestion, and neuralgia. Sometimes, people around me think I am tubercular when I cough too much. When the weather is bad my hip aches. Sometimes I can't open my eyes in the strong sunlight. I don't know the name of that disease. Also, our hands have many wounds from sewing.

I wonder if this is our destiny. Is poverty a sin, or is someone keeping us poor? Something must be wrong. Even if we work a whole day, we don't get paid for all the hours. If the manager asks us to do something, we just do it. We are ignorant and lazy.

Is ignorance a sin? No matter how our skills improve, no matter how hard we work, our lives have not been changed. The reality is the opposite. Life is becoming worse here day by day. Yet we don't have any idea how to avoid this.

The decay of public morals in this Peace Market can't be avoided. Ten years ago, when there were many houses of ill fame in Chong Kye chon and Change shin Dong, a lot of young girls who came from the countryside and had trouble making a living drifted here. These people entered factories and worked as shidas and then as operators. But their wages were terribly low and they had no place to live. They slept leaning against the wall in the hallway near the entrance to the factory. Finally almost all of these girls had to go to the amusement section of town. They made clothes in the daytime and stayed in unpermitted lodgings at night selling their bodies. Otherwise they couldn't support themselves.

How come it is so hard to live as this? Is it really such a hard thing to have three meals a day? Do people have to sell their bodies even to live? I wonder. No. To live should not be like that. The reason we are poor like this is that the owners have been exploiting us. In spite of economic development or modernization of our homeland, our pain has not been changed at all. I feel angry when someone says that people can make a living easier these days.

Work is an important thing to one's life. To eat good food and to play with pleasure should be combined with this. Work, which is basic, should be our greatest pleasure. Instead, we live such a painful life. We must sell our labor. It would be all right if we were paid fair wages, but we are not.

People have said recently that our government is spending money recklessly in the United States, England, Switzerland, and maybe Japan. Some king of an African country deposited a big amount of money in a bank in Switzerland. I hope powerful people in our country are not doing this. Anyone who felt free to do this should visit the Peace Market to look at us. How do they explain their using foreign goods, such as watches, glasses, ties, shoes, and their wives' clothes? Even the decoration of their houses, the plants in their gardens, and the goldfish in their ponds are all foreign. If they like foreign goods so much, they had better migrate to a foreign country. But I know they won't do it. Because they wouldn't be able to exploit the workers as they do here.

The people who are called economic scholars use "international competition" or some other difficult phrase when they talk. But we know they mean a way to squeeze workers' flesh and blood. Seen from this point of view, well-educated people are not always humane. According to Ms. Chong, some scholars have said that inflation can't be avoided for economic growth. What are they pursuing "economic growth" for? Inflation means the lowering of workers' wages and consumers being exploited. And if "economic growth" consists of the exploitation of people, including workers, it isn't necessary to grow economically. They simply disregard our hard life. I was surprised by Ms. Chong's explanation. People who lead, like scholars, are standing on the side of officials and owners.

To judge something is difficult. The same truth

looks different depending on where you stand. The scholars should stand on the side of the people in looking at export and economic development. People can't feel our pain without standing on our side. The only ones who can see and think from our point of view are ourselves. Only we know the pain. I feel that it is true that workers' rights will have to be acquired by workers.

Lucia

Lucia lives in the rich El Bahio region of central Mexico. The town is surrounded by huge farms owned by corporate firms. The men of the region find only seasonal work here because the farms are highly mechanized.

Throughout this region, production of export crops has displaced farming for domestic consumption, and the nutritional problems of the area are acute . . . 90 percent of the population suffers from nutritional deficiencies. Anemia is very common among women.

Lucia is landless and has no remunerable skills. She was dressed in ragged clothes and broken plastic sandals. Her eyes were those of a person who expects nothing but hardship in the years still ahead. Her skin was dark, and she covered her head and shoulders with a worn, green shawl.

I am fifty-five years old, and those years have not been good. I didn't even have shoes or many clothes. I was very, very poor. Every night I had to wash my clothes and then put them on again in the morning. I didn't have anything at all, just the fifteen children.

But only seven of my children are still living. The other eight died when they were babies. I think it was because of hunger. I was very weak while nursing them because we never had enough to eat. All we had was beans, beans, and more beans. Yes, it was the hunger that took the babies.

My husband was a laborer, but my mother-in-law kept the money. My husband was cruel with me. He beat me and screamed at me. He did many, many bad things. When he died, I sent the children to work as cattle herders. The owner of the cattle gives us some food. They eat better now.

Questions for Reflection

1. The questions below are ones asked by Min Chong Suk. They could as easily have been asked by Lucia and millions of others in our global family. In conversation with any of these sisters, how would you respond to these vital concerns?

Why are we now so poor and never able to escape?
Why is our life getting worse day by day?
Why can't we cut this dirty string?
Poor people should be united, but how?
If we were united could we make any change?
Is poverty a sin, or is someone keeping us poor?
How come it is so hard to live as this?

2. Min Chong Suk's questions point to the dead-end cyclical paths of those born into poverty. If you have enough money to buy this workbook, in all likelihood you were born into a different sort of situation. Compare your situation with your two sisters from the Third World. How do you explain why such different realities exist within one human family? Try to explain how the two different kinds of life situations interact to keep both intact.

3. Have you ever bought clothing made in Korea or Taiwan because it was attractive and less

expensive? How do you feel now about buying a blouse from Korea? Would it help or hurt women in Korea if you didn't? Think briefly about purchases you have made. Can you identify items that were less expensive for you because of low wages paid to those who produced them?

Getting in Touch with Some Beginning Answers

The selection that follows, from the pamphlet *Women in the Global Factory* by Annette Fuentes and Barbara Ehrenreich, is an extremely revealing and readable documented analysis that is vital to a more complete understanding of national and international economic issues.

Around the World with Multinational Corporations

In Penang, Malaysia, Julie K . . . looks good in the company's green-trimmed uniform and she's proud to work in a modern U.S.-owned factory. Not quite so proud as when she started working three years ago, she thinks, as she squints out the door at a passing group of women. All day at work, she peers through a microscope, bonding hair-thin gold wires to silicon chips that will end up inside pocket calculators. At twenty-one years of age, she is afraid she can no longer see very clearly.

In the 1800s, farm girls in England and the northeastern United States filled the textile mills of the first Industrial Revolution. Today, from Penang to Ciudad Juarez, young Third World women have become the new "factory girls," providing a vast pool of cheap labor for globetrotting corporations. Behind the labels "Made in Taiwan" and "Assembled in Haiti" may be one of the most strategic blocs of womanpower in the 1980s. In the last fifteen years, multinational corporations, such as Sears Roebuck and General Electric, have come to rely on women around the world to keep labor costs down and profits up. Women are the unseen assemblers of consumer goods such as toys and designer jeans, as well as the hardware of today's "Microprocessor Revolution."

Low wages are the main reason companies move to the Third World. A female assembly line worker in the United States is likely to earn between $3.10 and $5 an hour. In many Third World countries a woman doing the same work will earn $3 to $5 a *day.* Corporate executives, with their eyes glued to the bottom line, wonder why they should pay someone in Massachusetts on an hourly basis what someone in the Philippines will earn in a day. . . .

Table I. Cheap Labor (U.S. Dollars)

	Hourly Wage	Wages and Total of Fringe Benefits
Hong Kong	1.15	1.20
Singapore	.79	1.25
South Korea	.63	2.00
Taiwan	.53	.80
Malaysia	.48	.60
Philippines	.48	.50
Indonesia	.19	.35

Source: *Semiconductor International*, February 1982

U.S. corporations call their international production facilities "offshore sourcing." To unions these are "runaway shops" that take jobs away from American workers. Economists, meanwhile, talk about a "new international division of labor," in which low-skilled, labor-intensive jobs are shifted to the "newly industrializing" Third World countries. Control over management and technology, however, remains at company headquarters in First World countries like the United States and Japan. . . .

The pace of multinational production has accelerated rapidly since the mid-1960s. The electronics industry provides a good example of the new international division of labor: Circuits are printed on silicon wafers and tested in California; then the wafers are shipped to Asia for the labor-intensive process in which they are cut into tiny chips and bonded to circuit boards; final assembly into products such as calculators, video games, or military equipment usually takes place in the United States. Yet many American consumers don't realize that the goods they buy may have made a global journey and represent the labor of people in several countries—or that the "foreign" products that worry U.S. workers may have been made in factories owned, at least in part, by U.S. corporations.

History of the Global Factory

The Multinational Corporation. The sun never sets on it. . . . The profit motive has propelled it on a fantastic journey in search of new opportunities.
—*Irving Trust Company advertisement*

In a 1971 survey, "low wage rate" was the main reason corporations gave for choosing offshore sites. Fairchild Camera and Instrument Corporation was among the earliest to expand overseas; in 1961 it established an export production plant in Hong Kong where wages were about 28 cents an hour. More and more firms followed suit. Corporate executives rationalized their decision in terms of growing international competition: "Our major customer had bids from the Japanese and from American companies with offshore plants. We had to go abroad to compete."

Multinationals spread quickly in the 1960s, first to Hong Kong and Taiwan, next to South Korea and Mexico, and then Singapore and Malaysia, seeking ever cheaper production bases for the assembly of everything from baseballs to washing machines. From 1960 to 1969, investment in offshore manufacturing by U.S. firms mushroomed from $11.1 billion to $29.5 billion. In the mid-seventies Thailand and the Philippines became corporate favorites. The assembly line was stretching.

By moving overseas, corporations were able to escape U.S. and European trade union demands for more stringent health and safety standards as well as higher wages and benefits. The public's growing concern with industrial pollution could be neatly sidestepped by transferring the pollution to countries that had no environmental regulations. As a Malaysian Health Ministry doctor explained, "The government's policy is to attract investors. The first question an investor asks is: 'What regulations do you have, and how well do you enforce them?' If he finds these two areas are weak, he comes in."

During this period, earlier Third World economic development strategies—emphasizing the promotion of national industry and decreased dependence on imports from the U.S. and other Western countries—were scrapped for a new approach that, not coincidentally, fit the needs of multinational corporations. By 1965, export-led industrialization had become the favored strategy for development, touted by the United Nations Industrial Development Organization (UNIDO), the World Bank, and the International Monetary Fund (IMF), along with multinational corporations and banks. Third World countries were to roll out the red carpet for foreign investors and become "export platforms" producing goods for the world market. In return, "host governments" were promised jobs, technology, and foreign exchange (earnings in such international currencies as the dollar and mark, which are necessary for the purchase of imports such as oil and machinery). With assistance from UNIDO and the U.S. Agency for International Development (AID), "developing countries" designed their economies according to the multinational corporate blueprint. Protective trade barriers, of the kind used to protect U.S. and British industry in their fledgling years, were dropped to permit the "free flow" of capital and goods across national boundaries. Foreign investors were assured the full repatriation of their profits, and Third World governments outdid each other offering tax incentives. For companies that preferred not to own and operate factories offshore, subcontracting arrangements with local firms were encouraged as an alternative.

Free Trade Zones

Free trade zones (or export processing zones, as they are also known) have emerged as key elements in this export-led development. The free trade zone is a haven for foreign investment, complete with electricity and other infrastructure and a labor force often housed in nearby dormitories. It is a colonial-style economic order, tailor-made for multinational corporations. Customs-free import of raw materials, components, and equipment, tax holidays of up to twenty years, and government subsidization of operating costs are some of the enticements to investment. National firms are usually prohibited from operating in the zones unless they invest jointly with a foreign company.

Free trade zones—there are now over 100—mean more freedom for business and less freedom for people. Inside, behind walls often topped with barbed wire, the zones resemble a huge labor camp where trade unions, strikes, and freedom of movement are severely limited, if not forbidden. A special police force is on hand to search people and vehicles entering or leaving the zones.

According to a highly placed Third World woman within the United Nations, "The multinationals like to say they're contributing to development, but they come into our countries for one thing—cheap labor. If the labor stops being so cheap, they can move on. So how can you call that development? It depends on the people being poor and staying poor."

Puerto Rico's "Operation Bootstrap," which began in the late 1940s, was a preview of the free trade zone model of "development." The Puerto Rican Economic Development Administration placed an advertisement in U.S. newspapers in 1976, appealing for corporate investment with the promise, "You're in good company in Puerto Rico, U.S.A.," where there are "higher productivity, lower wages, and tax-free profits." But companies aren't necessarily good for Puerto Rico. Under "Operation Bootstrap," export production increased as production of domestic necessities declined. In 1982, unemployment topped 30 percent; the island of Puerto Rico, with its tropical climate and fertile soil, now imports almost all of its food as well as manufactured goods from the "mainland." To pay for these costly imports, the country has gone into debt to U.S. banks and other lending agencies. In

1976, when the initial tax "holidays" for foreign investors ran out and minimum wage laws were implemented, many companies left to exploit even cheaper labor in Haiti and the Dominican Republic. . . .

A nimble seamstress, twenty-three-year-old veteran Basillia Altagracia, eventually began to earn as much as $5.75 a day in the Dominican Republic's La Romana free trade zone. . . . "I was exceeding my piecework quota by a lot." . . . But then, Altagracia said, her plant supervisor, a Cuban émigré, called her into his office. "He said I was doing a fine job, but that I and some other of the women were making too much money, and he was being forced to lower what we earned for each piece we sewed." On the best days, she now can clear barely $3, she said. "I was earning less, so I started working six and seven days a week. But I was tired and I could not work as fast as before." Within a few months she was too ill to work at all.

AFL-CIO American Federationist

There are over one million people employed in industrial free trade zones in the Third World. Millions more work outside the zones in multinational-controlled plants and domestically owned subcontracting factories. Eighty to ninety percent of the light-assembly workers are women. This is a remarkable switch from earlier patterns of foreign-controlled industrialization. Until recently, economic development involved heavy industries such as mining and construction and usually meant more jobs for men and—compared to traditional agricultural society—a diminished economic status for women. But multinationals consider light-assembly work, whether the product is Barbie dolls or computer components, to be women's work.

Women everywhere are paid lower wages than men. Since multinationals go overseas to reduce labor costs, women are the natural choice for assembly jobs. Wage-earning opportunities for women are limited, and women are considered only supplementary income earners for their families. Management uses this secondary status to pay women less than men and justify layoffs during slow periods, claiming that women don't need to work and will probably quit to get married anyway.

Women are the preferred workforce for other reasons. Multinationals want a workforce that is docile, easily manipulated, and willing to do boring, repetitive assembly work. Women, they claim, are the perfect employees, with their "natural patience" and "manual dexterity." As the personnel manager of an assembly plant in Taiwan says, "Young male workers are too restless and impatient to be doing monotonous work with no career value. If displeased they sabotage the machines and even

threaten the foreman. But girls, at most they cry a little."

Multinationals prefer single women with no children and no plans to have any. Pregnancy tests are routinely given to potential employees to avoid the issue of maternity benefits. In India, a woman textile worker reports that "they do take unmarried women but they prefer women who have had an operation," referring to her government's sterilization program. In the Philippines' Bataan Export Processing Zone the Mattel toy company offers prizes to workers who undergo sterilization.

Third World women haven't always been a ready workforce. Until two decades ago, young women were vital to the rural economy in many countries. They worked in the home, in agriculture, or in local cottage industries. But many Third World governments adopted development plans favoring large-scale industry and agribusiness as advocated by such agencies as the World Bank and the International Monetary Fund. Traditional farming systems and communities are now crumbling as many families lose their land and local enterprises collapse. As a result of the breakdown of the rural economy, many families now send their daughters to the cities or the free trade zones in an attempt to assure some income.

The majority of the new female work force is young, between sixteen and twenty-five years old. As one management consultant explains, "When seniority rises, wages rise," so the companies prefer to train a fresh group of teenagers rather than give experienced women higher pay. Different industries have different age and skill standards. The youngest workers, usually under twenty-three years old, are found in electronics and textile factories where keen eyesight and dexterity are essential. A second, older group of women work in industries like food processing where nimble fingers and perfect vision aren't required. Conditions in these factories are particularly bad. Multinationals can get away with more because the women generally can't find jobs elsewhere. . . .

Corporate apologists are quick to insist that Third World women are absolutely thrilled with their newfound employment. . . .

Third World governments are often willing partners in the exploitation of working women. The government treasuries gain little direct revenue from this kind of investment, because of all the financial incentives they offer. But host governments can count on economic and military assistance from the United States and other Western countries and receive loans from multinational banks and lending agencies. Government officials enrich themselves by specializing in cutting red tape for an "agent's fee" or an outright bribe, and Harvard- or Berkeley-educated technocrats assume a privileged niche as local managers.

In the competition for corporate investment, prospective host governments advertise women shamelessly. The Royal Thai embassy sends U.S. businesses a brochure guaranteeing that, in Thailand, "the relationship between the employer and the employee is like that of a guardian and a ward. It is easy to win and maintain the loyalty of workers as long as they are treated with kindness and courtesy." The facing page offers a highly selective photo study of Thai women: giggling shyly, bowing submissively, and working cheerfully on an assembly line.

Many governments are willing to back up their advertising with whatever amount of repression it takes to keep "their girls" as docile as they appear in the brochures. A feature of martial law in the Philippines, for example, is the New Labor Code, which President Marcos instituted to stifle increasing labor unrest. The code bans all strikes in "vital industries," including all industries in the export processing zones, and permits companies to suspend any worker "who poses a serious danger to the life or property of the employer," a statute that is frequently interpreted to block all forms of labor activism.

Even the most moderate and orderly attempts to organize are likely to bring down heavy doses of police brutality. In Guatemala, in 1975, women workers in a U.S. factory producing jeans and jackets drew up a list of complaints that included insults by management, piecework wages that were less than the legal minimum, no overtime pay, and "threats of death." The U.S. boss made a quick call to the local authorities to report that he was being harassed by "Communists." When the women reported to work the next day they found the factory surrounded by heavily armed contingents of military police. The "Communist" organizers were identified and fired. . . .

The most powerful promoter of exploitative conditions for Third World women workers is the U.S. government. The notorious South Korean textile industry was developed with $400 million in U.S. aid. Malaysia became a low-wage haven for the electronics industry with assistance from the U.S. Agency for International Development. Taiwan's status as a "showcase for the Free World" and a comfortable berth for multinational corporations is the result of three decades of U.S. economic and military support.

Non-governmental agencies work directly with AID and the State Department or covertly with the CIA to cultivate support and derail opposition in Third World countries. For example, the AFL-CIO's Asian-American Free Labor Institute (AAFLI) ostensibly works to encourage "free" (read "procapitalist") trade unions in Asia, but its acutal mission is to discourage progressive, mass-based worker activity. AAFLI is very active in the Philippines and works with the Federation of Korean Trade Unions. . . . In Latin America, the American Institute for Free Labor Development (AIFLD) serves the same purpose, co-opting or destroying genuine worker organizing attempts.

The most blatant form of U.S. involvement, explains Lenny Siegel, director of the Pacific Studies Center, is "our consistent record of military aid to Third World governments that are capitalist, politically repressive, and not striving for economic independence." Thailand has been ruled by a military junta since 1976. Singapore's dictator Lee Kuan Yew took power in 1959, repressing students, unionists, leftists, and the media. Indonesia's bloody 1965 coup ushered in the regime of Suharto, who placed strict controls on labor organizing, including the banning of strikes. Malaysia has labor ordinances restricting unionization, and the unions which do exist are weak and ineffective.

"Hospitality Girls"

The growth of multinational enterprises in East Asia is directly tied to the rise of tourism and the "hospitality industry," a euphemism for organized prostitution, employing thousands of women. An advertisement for the Rosie Travel Company in Thailand reads:

> Thailand is a world full of extremes and the possibilities are unlimited. Anything goes in this exotic country. Especially when it comes to girls. Still, it appears to be a problem for visitors to Thailand to find the right places where they can indulge in unknown pleasures. Rosie has done something about this. For the first time in history you can book a trip to Thailand with erotic pleasures included in the price.

For Noi, a twenty-year-old Thai woman, prostitution provides a desperately needed second income. "I get 25 *baht* per day" [then worth less than $1.50] working in a battery factory, she explains. "But this is not enough to cover my expenses. How could this be enough to pay for my food, my bus ticket, and other expenses? And I can tell you I am thrifty. I have to find work at night so that I can send money to my parents." Many other prostitutes are former factory workers, desperate for employment, or young women who come to the cities looking for factory work they never found.

In the Philippines, tourism is part of the government's strategy for development; it is the country's fourth largest source of foreign exchange. Its success stems from its "hospitality industry," which caters to male tourists, primarily from Japan. Officially, there are about 100,000 "hostesses," representing those women who have received government permits to work in licensed businesses, such as bars and cafés. But an accurate figure must include streetwalkers, call girls, and brothel workers, none of whom are registered with the government. . . .

Tourism is also a big industry in South Korea, with revenues of $270 million a year. *Kiasaeng* (prostitutes) are responsible for this success. Although the Law on Decadent Acts includes a strict anti-prostitution code, *kiasaeng* are regularly issued ID cards by the government to allow them into tourist areas to work. . . .

The Answer Is Global

Women all over the world are becoming a giant reserve army of labor at the disposal of globetrotting multinations. No woman can feel job security on the assembly line as long as the profit motive guides multinational activities. Runaways are now occurring *within* the Third World. Sri Lanka, which recently opened an export processing zone, has become a haven for companies fleeing the labor militancy in South Korea and the Philippines. . . .

With the continued economic crisis, when even low-paid jobs are hard to come by, it is especially easy for companies to play off their employees against each other. As sociologist Cynthia Enloe says, "We're all being fed the line that we are each other's competitors." Women in a Tennessee garment factory are threatened with competition from Mexican workers, while women in the Philippines are threatened with competition from Sri Lanka. It's a competition in which all workers are losers; wages are driven down everywhere, and health and safety conditions deteriorate, but job security is never achieved. . . .

Rachel Grossman, a specialist on Southeast Asia, argues, "Protectionism and nationalist attitudes that view Third World imports and workers as competition are lagging behind the times. The international nature of production has been an economic reality for some time now. Multinationals don't deal in terms of individual countries, but on a global scale." Any strategy to further women's control over their work lives must take into account that new economic reality. Saralee Hamilton, coordinator of the AFSC Nationwide Women's Program, says, "The multinational corporations have deliberately targeted women for exploitation. If feminism is going to mean anything to women all over the world, it's going to have to find new ways to resist corporate power internationally." . . .

The most difficult yet most important task in confronting multinational domination is to create direct links between women workers around the world. International travel is expensive, and few women have the money for long-distance phone calls or even postage. But some links are being made, such as UE's developing relationship with KMU of the Philippines. The Nationwide Women's Program organized a conference in 1978 on women and global corporations which brought together women from the Third World and the United States to share information and ideas. Out of that conference came the Women and Global Corporations project which encourages networking of working women in the Third World with women in the Western countries to provide support for their common struggles.

It may take years before international links are extensive and powerful enough successfully to challenge multinational corporations and the governments which support them, but women's lives grow closer all the time. "We all have the same hard life," wrote Min Chong Suk. "We are bound together with one string."

Now turn back to Min Chong Suk's questions. Is there additional information you would want to add to your answers?

Summarize your findings by completing the following sentence: The primary purpose of our present economic system seems to be —————.

Women, Hierarchy, Work, and Economics

In this section, we will be looking more specifically at the nature, meaning, and purpose of work and the place this activity has within an economic system.

Reflections on Western Culture and Work Activities

In *Green Paradise Lost* (pp. 19–20), author Elizabeth Gray uses the analogy of eyeglasses to illustrate how cultural conditioning determines how we perceive and understand life experiences. "These eyeglasses are the mental models or paradigms we use; as such, they constitute our culturally generated and shared basic interpretations of life." Describing a basic set of glasses of Western culture, she says:

When seen through this lens, reality is like a ladder or pyramid—"a great chain of being"—in which everything is either up or down, dominant or subordinate, superior or inferior, better or worse. . . . [W]hen we are responding to differences (whether man or woman, or man and whale . . . or man and God), our perceptions are dominated and distorted by the hierarchical paradigm. Almost in the same instant that we perceive difference, we are looking to ascertain rankings of power, moral or economic value, and aesthetic preference. We do this whether it is a different animal, a different culture, or a skin pigmentation that is different.

The hierarchical paradigm is thus not simply an ordinary eyeglass. . . . It is a veritable contact lens. So intimately is it a part of how we perceive that we seem never to assess difference as just that—different. Instead we insist upon imposing comparative rankings which are incomplete and often self-serving.

Perhaps more important, we have in our Western tradition perceived what is different as "the Other." . . . And we have always set immediately to work ranking ourselves against that Other. If that Other is God, He is above me—superior. If that Other is female (and I am male), she is below me—inferior. If that Other is animal, I am superior because I am more complex, more "highly developed," or because I am "created in the image and likeness of God." If that Other is another culture, it is probably below me because I do not understand it but at first glance it seems "more primitive," "less complex," or simply less powerful.

Later, Gray adds:

Man has wanted to see himself as the creator and experiencer of history and culture—set apart from objects (lesser men, women, slaves, nature, things) which he could act upon, observe, and manipulate with detachment as though "above" and "apart." What I am saying is that reality is not . . . partitioned. It is not hierarchical. It does not consist of builders and building blocks, observers and observed, doers and done-to. Reality is a complex and dynamic web of energy and relationships which simply includes the human, both female and male.

Although Gray does not deal with how our cultural eyeglasses affect the way we perceive different kinds of work, it is true that they do. We compare and then rank some work as being "better" or "higher" than other kinds, and we reward accordingly. Our arrangement of work activities reflects a hierarchical scale.

Questions for Reflection

1. Take a few minutes and construct a ladder of jobs, with those least respected at the bottom and those most highly respected at the top. Where does "traditional women's work" fall on your ladder?

2. What reasons have been used to justify such grading of work activities?

3. What would happen if our culture started valuing (shown by amount of respect and reward given) all work activities equally?

4. Can you think of reasons for not arranging work activities hierarchically?

Entering Into the Story of Another

Ramona Bennett

Do you know we're on a reservation at this moment? It was reserved forever for the members of my tribe. "Forever" meant until some white people wanted it. I'm a member of the Puyallup tribe. It's called that by the whites because they couldn't pronounce our foreign name: Spalallapubsh. (Laughs.)

We were a fishing people. We had camps all the way from McNeill's Island to Salmon Bay and clear up to Rodando. In 1854, agents of the United States government met with our people and did a treaty. They promised us they only needed land to farm. They assured us that our rights as commercial fishing people would not be disturbed. Because Indian people have always been generous, we agreed to share.

Our tribes were consolidated onto this reservation, twenty-nine thousand acres. We lost eleven thousand in the survey, so we came down to eighteen thousand. We should have known, but we're a trusting people.

We were long-house people, matriarchal, where the whole extended family lived together. We didn't have real estate problems. There was lots of space for everybody, so we didn't have to stand our long houses on end and call them skyscrapers.

The white people decided we'd make good farmers, so they separated our long-house families into forty-, eighty-, and 160-acre tracts. If we didn't improve our land, we'd lose it. They really knew it wouldn't work, but it was a way of breaking up our society. Phil Lucas, who's a beautiful Indian folk singer, says the marriage between the non-Indians and the Indians was a perfect one. The Indian measures his success by his ability to share. The white man measures his importance by how much he can take. There couldn't have been two more perfect cultures to meet, with the white people taking everything and the Indians giving everything.

They then decided that because we couldn't read or write or speak English, we should all be assigned guardians. So the lawyers and judges and police and businessmen who came out with Milwaukee Railroad and Weyerhaeuser Lumber, all these good citizens were assigned their fair share of Indians to be guardians for. They sold the land to each other, kept the money for probate fees, and had the sheriffs come out and remove any Indians still living on this land. Those Indians unwilling to be removed were put on the railroad tracks and murdered. We became landless on our own reservations.

The kids were denied access to anything traditionally theirs. They had programs called Domestic Science, where little Indian girls were taught how to wash dishes for white people, cook meals for white people, mop floors for white people. If they were very, very smart, they were taught how to be beauticians and cut white people's hair, or to be waitresses and serve white people in restaurants, to be clerk typists, maybe, and type white people's ideas. All the boys went through a program called Agricultural Science, where they were taught how to plow white people's fields and take care of white people's cows and chickens and to care for the produce that was being raised on their own land,

stolen by non-Indians. If these boys were very, very smart, they were taught to be unemployed welders or unemployed sheet-metal workers. People that do the hiring are whites, and they tend to be more comfortable with people who resemble them. . . .

In school, I learned the same lies you learned: that Columbus discovered America, that there were no survivors at Little Big Horn, that the first baby born west of the Mississippi was born to Narcissa Whitman. All the same crap that you learned, I learned. Through those movies, I learned that an Irishman who stands up for his rights is a patriot, and an Indian who stands up for his rights is a savage. I learned that the pioneers made the West a fit place for decent folks to live. I learned that white people had to take land away from the Indian people because we didn't know how to use it. It wasn't plowed, logged, and paved. It wasn't strip-mined. It had to be taken from us because we had no environmental knowledge or concerns. We were just not destructive enough to be considered *really* civilized.

. . . I know damn good and well that if American children in school had learned that the beautiful Cheyenne women at Sand Creek put their shawls over their babies' faces so they wouldn't see the long knives, if the American schoolchildren learned that Indian mothers held their babies close to their bodies when the Gatling guns shot and killed three hundred, there would never have been a My Lai massacre. If the history teacher had really been truthful with American children, Calley would have given an order to totally noncooperating troops. There would have been no one to fight. There would have been a national conscience. The lie has made for an American nightmare, not dream. . . .

I met a bunch of Eskimos from Alaska that the Methodists got hold of. They call it the Methodist ethic. If you work, you're good, if you don't, you're bad. I don't impose that ethic on other people. These Eskimos are now so task-oriented, they're very, very hyper. They don't know how to relax. The Methodists got hold of their heads, and they lost what they had. They're in a mad dash all the time and don't know how to sit and cogitate.

My little six-year-old will go out, just sit and talk to one of those trees or observe the birds. He can be calm and comfortable doing that. He hasn't been through the same brainwash that the rest of us have.

There's a knowledge born in these little ones that ties back to the spirit world, to the Creator. Those little kids in school can tell you that the nations of fish are their brothers and sisters. They'll tell you that their life is no more important than the life of that animal or that tree or that flower. They're born knowing that. It's that our school doesn't beat it out of them. . . .

My little son shares the continent with 199,999,999 other folks. (Laughs.) If your government screws up and creates one more damned war, his little brown ass will get blown away, right along with all your people. All those colors (laughs) and all those attitudes. The bombs that come don't give a damn if he's got cute little braids, is a little brown boy, talks to cedar trees, and is a sweet little person. . . . We're all in the same canoe.

Questions

1. List the economic injustices that are pointed out in Ramona's story. How did whites justify these injustices?

2. What different views of the meaning and importance of work activities do you identify in this story?

3. According to Ramona, why are some kinds of work activities valued more than others?

4. How is it decided what kinds of activities are needed in society? How is it decided and who decides who will do what and who will train for what?

5. What relationships are identified between violence, racism, sexism, and a hierarchical view of human differences (that some kinds of persons and ways of life are of more value than others)?

Getting in Touch with Your Present

Use the "Economic Consciousness Razors" that follow to reflect on the role of economics in your present life. All questions may not be applicable to your particular situation, but all may trigger some thoughts as to your past, present, or future participation in economic life.

Just as you wrote your past economic history in Section 1, now write your recent economic history. After you have finished, read the Fact Sheet on Women and Work that follows and see if there are any additions you might like to make to your statement.

Economic Consciousness Razors

1. How and by whom was the decision made that you would do the kind of work you are presently involved in? What is the primary reason you work: Enjoyment? For self-fulfillment? Love? To meet the needs of family or society? Self-worth? To make a living? Another reason?

2. If you were trained for that work, how and by whom was the decision made about the kind of training and education you would receive? What was the primary reason this particular training was chosen?

3. In your adult life, have you ever worked primarily to be self-supporting, or have you always been contributing to your paternal or maternal household bills? Of all the siblings in your family, who takes on the largest share of this filial responsibility?

4. Are you single and self-supporting? If so, how do you make decisions about how your income is spent? Are you presently using a portion of your income to ensure that you can, if need be, always (even in retirement) be self-supporting? If so, what portion of your income goes into that sort of "securing" of the present and future?

5. Do you share household expenses? Are you an unpaid homemaker or wife and mother? Do you do that work in addition to a regular job? If so, who earns more, you or your mate? What kind of job do you do, for what sort of employer? Do you plan to stay in this line of work for a while, or are you treading water while your mate moves up or around in his employment plans?

6. Are you economically responsible for children? How has this affected your relation to your work and your attitude about jobs?

7. How has the current economic situation affected your household? Has your income grown to be a larger share of total household bills?

8. Who makes the decisions in your household about how money is spent? Do your children participate in these decisions? Does the money that you earn go to some things and the money that your mate earns go to others? Whose income is earmarked for investment in financial security or for educational opportunity for your children?

9. Can you think of ways in which your office or workplace is structured like an economic family? In terms of who makes resource-allocation decisions, who gives orders to whom or who asks whom to do what, how tasks, status, and pay are divided among the people who work there?

10. How have the current economic problems in the United States been felt differently by men and women at your workplace? By younger workers and older workers? Were women or younger people "excessed" more quickly than men? Or were men's jobs threatened first, assuming their salaries are a greater cost to the employer?

11. If you live in a religious community where all expenses are shared among a group of women, can you talk about how your relation to jobs and your attitude about money have differed from those of women whose lives are intertwined in more traditional economic family structures? How have the economic roles in your community changed over the last twenty-five years? What future economic plans does your community hold?

12. What do you think is God's intended purpose of work?

Fact Sheet on Women and Work

1. The majority of women work because of economic need. In 1982 there were 110 million people in the civilian labor force in the United States. This figure represents a gain of 26.6 percent, or 23 million workers, since 1972. Women account for 62 percent of that growth. In July 1983 there were 48.5 million employed women (nearly half of all women), and they accounted for 44 percent of the total labor force (as compared with 40 percent in 1981). A Labor Department projection indicates that women will account for seven out of ten additions to the labor force during the 1980s.

A survey by the Harris polling firm reported in the July 1984 *Ms.* magazine asked women what their attitude toward work outside the home would be if they "had enough money to live as comfortably" as they would like. Nineteen percent said they would continue full-time work, 30 percent preferred to work part-time, 14 percent said they would do volunteer work, and 35 percent wanted to work at home caring for their families.

2. Within the 43 million working women are 51 percent of all married women, 62 percent of all single never-married women, and 45 percent of all divorced, widowed, and separated women. Table II shows the increase in the proportion of women working in the last decade.

3. The more education a woman has, the greater the likelihood that she will seek paid employment. Among the women with four or more years of college, about three out of five (58 percent) were in the labor force in 1981. In 1982, about 81 percent of all working women were high school graduates, as compared with 77 percent of all working men. Almost 17 percent of working women are college graduates, as compared with 21 percent of working men.

Table II. Increase in Proportion of Women Working

	% of Married Women		% of Divorced, Widowed, and Separated Women	
	Children under 18	Children under 6	Children under 18	Children under 6
1972	41	30	59	47
1982	56	49	70	61
% Increase	34	52	74	59

College enrollment for all women has increased by 60 percent in the past decade. In 1982, there were 6.4 million women enrolled, as compared with 6 million men. In 1981, women workers with four or more years of college had about the same income as men who had only one to three years of high school: $12,085 and $11,936, respectively. When employed full-time year round, women high school graduates had about the same average income as men who had not completed elementary school: $12,332 and $12,866, respectively.

4. Although the general educational achievements of working women are on a par with those of working men, the median earnings of year-round full-time working women in 1982 was substantially less than the median income of men in the same job categories—60 percent less, an actual decrease from just over 60 percent in 1981 (Table III).

In 1982, women performed approximately two thirds of the paid and unpaid labor, received 10 percent of the paid income, and owned 1 percent of the property. In addition, as shown by the July 1984 *Ms.* article, among working couples the men spent an average of 12.6 hours a week on family care and the women about 24.8 hours. At the same time, men averaged 41.6 hours of paid work to women's 38.4 hours. This breakdown averages 117.4 hours per week per couple, or the equivalent of a three-job family, the woman working 63.2 hours and the man 54.2 hours.

5. In 1983, women were still concentrated in low-paying dead-end jobs and traditional occupations. In 1981 women were 80 percent of all clerical workers but only 6 percent of all craft workers; 62 percent of service workers but only 45 percent of professional and technical workers, and 63 percent of retail sales workers but only 28 percent of nonfarm managers and administrators. Over 80 percent of working women are concentrated in sales, service, clerical, crafts, light manufacturing, or similar jobs. While white women have about twenty occupations open to them, women of color are still basically limited to two: clerical and service, earning an average of 54 cents to every dollar earned by white men in comparative jobs. At the same time, low-paying jobs are increasing while high-paying jobs are decreasing. Women's "ghetto jobs" are increasing by 70 percent (fast food jobs, sweatshops hiring undocumented workers and piecework in the home) are all on the increase. This trend indicates that women are being identified as a low labor group.

6. In 1982, it was reported that 90 percent of women in private industry retire with no pension plan. Those with a pension get an average of $80 a month. The average unmarried working woman retires with less than $1,000 in the bank. One out of three women in the work force were forty-five years and older. Many of these older women are the sole support of themselves and their dependents.

In addition, while many employees think their pension rights will automatically go to their surviving spouse, many companies have strict age eligibility laws and require signature agreements. Homemakers often find themselves ineligible for Social Security because of divorce or the absence of a husband's signature. Women who buy pensions and annuities are also subject to discrimination in the prices they are charged, even if they are of the same age and occupational status as their male counterparts.

Only about 59 percent of divorced women with children at home were awarded child support in 1981, but census bureau statistics show that 25 percent of these women received only partial payment and 28 percent received no payment at all. The average annual child-support payment was $2,106, and the average total income of women receiving child support was $11,747. In 1982, Social Security payments averaged only $233 per month for a single woman. This was 85 percent of the total income of the majority of elderly women, who make up 70 percent of all poor people over age sixty-five.

The unemployment rate was lowest for adult white men (twenty and over) and highest for young black women (sixteen to nineteen), according to the 1981 figures from the Department of Labor (Table IV). After the age of forty, unemployment rates are one third higher for women than men.

Older women experience longer periods of unemployment when compared to younger women. A half million working women work part-time involuntarily because they cannot find full-time employment.

Mary Rubin, a research associate for the Business and Professional Women's Foundation, conducted a policy analysis in the fall of 1981. In her report, *Women and Poverty,* she concluded:

> Woman's employment and women's poverty go hand in hand. Women's poverty is best understood as women who are underpaid and employed in dead-end jobs rather than poor people who *happen* to be women. The current [1982] budget cuts hit women disproportionately hard, but this is not new. . . . Women have always faced poverty. We need public policies that start with the assumption that women need and want to be able to support themselves and their families.

The Global Picture

The foregoing facts refer only to women in the United States. We must remember that for women throughout the world the situation is generally more drastic. When the United Na-

Table III. Median Earnings in 1982 for Full-Time Workers, by Race

OCCUPATION	WHITE		BLACK		HISPANICS	
	Women	Men	Women	Men	Women	Men
Executives, Administrators, and Managerial	$17,518	$30,388	$17,403	$21,008	$16,761	$22,673
Professional Specialty Occupations	18,307	27,712	16,747	20,265	15,187	27,392
Technicians and Related	15,399	22,472	14,218	14,502	13,589	19,285
Sales	11,253	22,819	10,466	15,318	9,963	17,640
Administrative Support	12,920	20,870	12,814	17,226	12,384	14,776
Service	9,080	15,169	9,523	12,500	8,350	11,942
Craftsmen and Repairers	13,960	21,807	15,793	17,033	11,448	16,918
Operations and Laborers	10,955	17,665	11,305	15,041	8,969	14,154
Farming, Forestry, Fishing	7,764	12,102	8,245	8,129	6,466	10,813
TOTAL	$13,520	$22,149	$12,355	$15,596	$11,261	$15,446

tions was founded, only a third of the 51 member nations had granted political rights to women. Presently all but 8 of the 149 member states have granted women's suffrage by law, but in most areas of the world these protections do not in fact ensure equality—especially economic equality.

Table IV. Unemployment Rate 1981

Adults	Percent	Teenagers	Percent
White men	5.6	White women	16.6
White women	5.9	White men	17.9
Hispanic men	8.8	Hispanic men	23.3
Hispanic women	9.5	Hispanic women	24.5
Black women	13.4	Black men	40.7
Black men	13.5	Black women	42.2

As Patricia Mische has noted, in an April 1982 "Sociomemo" from the Office of Social Ministry in Richmond, Virginia, excerpted from *The Whole Earth Papers*:

In most areas of the world, despite some progress, women continue to be educationally, economically, and politically disadvantaged or discriminated against. For instance: Of the approximately 800 million illiterates round the world, nearly two thirds are women. In some countries women account for as much as 80 to 85 percent of illiteracy. Women in many countries are the central figures in agriculture, food preparation, health care, nutrition, children's welfare, population control, and other vital areas related to a nation's economic development and well-being. Yet women had been all but forgotten in development planning during the first United National development decade of the 60's. Efforts to rectify this omission were made in the second development decade of the 70's, but there is still a long way to go in achieving greater participation of women.

In many countries, women constitute one third or more of all heads of households and are the sole support of their families and even extended families. Yet in rich and poor countries, women find themselves concentrated in a limited number of jobs, frequently at low levels of skill and responsibility and with equally low wages. Women also find themselves handicapped in obtaining credit, mortgage loans, insurance, tax benefits, and other economic benefits.

Women have discovered that to make progress in other areas of women's rights and needs, they need to have more women in positions of political leadership. But, in most countries and in the United Nations, women have few positions of leadership, and these tend to decrease as the center of power is approached. For example, there are presently two women heads of state, and there have been only five in this century. In the United States, women have had political rights by law for over fifty years, but they hold only 5 percent of public offices. In the United Nations, women's equality is a charter mandate, but few women are in top positions.

After preparing your recent economic history and reading the information in the Fact Sheet on Women and Work, be aware of how your body is feeling. Does it give you some clues about your response to this information? Now complete the following sentences:

Thinking about these realities makes me feel —————.

As a result, I would like to —————.

PART TWO
Biblical Roots

SECTION 4

The Jesus Movement and Economics

In this section, we will explore biblical roots of the Jesus movement and enter that movement through imaginative involvement in order to determine the linkage between the Christian faith and economic realities and to discover how Jewish women (our fore-sisters) who followed Jesus expressed that linkage in their life situations.

Reflections on the Role of Women

An early statement about those who followed Jesus highlights the inclusive nature of this community.

> Soon afterward he went on through cities and villages, preaching and bringing the good news of the kingdom of God. And the twelve were with him, and also some women who had been healed of evil spirits and infirmities: Mary, called Magdalene, from whom seven demons had gone out, and Joanna, the wife of Chuza, Herod's steward, and Susanna, and many others, who provided for them out of their means.
>
> (Luke 8:1–3)

Such an inclusive community may not seem unusual to us today, but for Jesus' time it was extraordinary, because women were viewed as lesser creatures than men in both Judaism and the Greco-Roman culture. Indeed, in many respects in Judaism, the woman was seen as the property of her father or husband, many of whom thanked God three times daily for not having been created a Gentile, a slave, or a woman. As Sheila Collins remarks in *A Different Heaven and Earth* (p. 65),

> Not only was woman secondary, but because of the superstition about menstrual blood and the earthiness of childbirth, she was ritually unclean, having to spend great periods of her life in seclusion. By law and custom women were excluded from both the privileges and responsibilities of religious life. Only males could speak to and for God, and only males were rightful inheritors of the Jewish name and tradition—the true Israelites.

In order more fully to understand the implications of Jesus' ministry, not only for women but also for economic arrangements, one should know something of the historical period into which Jesus came. It was a turbulent time in which the Jewish people's political and economic independence had once again been destroyed. Life under Roman rule included an ever-present occupation army and extremely heavy taxation of every item, activity, and operation. These factors led to insurrections and protests instigated by rebellious and proud Jews. Sharecroppers, absentee landowners with intermediate debt collectors, slavery, corrupt tax collectors, cruel punishment for anticipated or real acts of subversion, and severe hostility between Jew and Gentile were daily facts of life. There was no middle class as we know it. Rather, there was the extreme prosperity and wealth of the few existing alongside the poverty and illness of the masses. Elisabeth Schüssler Fiorenza (*In Memory of Her,* p. 141) says that

> in the first century—as today—the majority of the poor and starving were women, especially those women who had no male agencies that might enable them to share in the wealth of the patriarchal system. In antiquity widows and orphans were the prime paradigms of the poor and exploited.

Temple and synagogue were situated in close proximity to a rapidly growing number of gymnasiums and theaters for the affluent. Cultural and religious confusion prevailed, as did economic uncertainty. Mid-East Gentiles, Greeks, Romans, and pagans—all had divergent attitudes toward the poor. There was also considerable ferment within Judaism itself, because the social, economic, and religious laws and attitudes of the Hebrews had arisen out of a radically different national and cultural situation. The tensions within Judaism were reflected in different Jewish parties (Sadducees, Pharisees, Zealots, Essenes), who had divergent understandings of Judaism itself and often expressed conflicting ideas about how the Jewish community should relate and respond not just to the outcast, the lower class, and the poor but their foreign rulers as well. It was into this sort of setting that Jesus came, preaching the good news of an inclusive, liberating, caring community.

> And he came to Nazareth, . . . and he went to the synagogue, as his custom was, on the sabbath

day. And he stood up to read; and there was given to him the book of the prophet Isaiah. He opened the book and found the place where it was written,

> "The Spirit of the Lord is upon me,
>   because he has anointed me to preach
>   good news to the poor.
> He has sent me to proclaim release
>   to the captives
> and recovering of sight to the blind,
> to set at liberty those who are oppressed,
> to proclaim the acceptable year
>   of the Lord."
>
> (Luke 4:16–19)

This year was generally associated with the Jubilee vision, a time when slaves were set free, debts were remitted, and, most importantly, land was equitably redistributed.

These words were used to announce Jesus' ministry. Responding to Jesus' announcement in act as well as word, the followers of Jesus entered a new kind of family, which included those who had been marginalized from society. As Fiorenza points out (p. 130):

> In the ministry of Jesus, God is experienced as all-inclusive love. . . . This God is a God of graciousness and goodness who accepts everyone and brings about justice and well-being for everyone without exception. The creator God accepts all members of Israel, and especially the impoverished, the crippled, the outcast, the sinner and prostitutes, as long as they are prepared to engage in the perspective and power of the *basileia* [kingdom].

Questions for Reflection

1. Imagine yourself in the world of Jesus' ministry. How does Jesus' exceptional acceptance of *you* as a disciple make you feel about yourself? your family?

2. How does this acceptance affect the way you feel about and relate to other women? Men? Other former outcasts to the mainstream of life?

3. What do you want to do in response to your new inclusion in a community of equals?

Entering Into the Stories of Others

Imagine yourself to be a part of that group of early followers of Jesus who "were of one heart and soul" and decided to do away with private property (Acts 4:32) and to sell "their possessions and goods," to share "all things in common," and to distribute "them to all, as any had need" (Acts 2:44–45).

Keep in mind the fact that as a woman you are not a marginal participant but can exercise full leadership, as was true in the early Christian community. See Elisabeth Schüssler Fiorenza, "Women in the Early Christian Movement," in *Womanspirit Rising: A Feminist Reader in Religion,* edited by Carol P. Christ and Judith Plaskow, pages 84–92. Also see Mark 15:40–41; Luke 24:10; Acts 2:17; 16:14; 17:4, 12; 21:9–14; Col. 4:15; Philemon 2; etc.

Now write an account of a conversation you have had with a woman presently outside the Christian community. Tell her about the role you played in coming to the decision about sharing resources recorded in Acts 2:41–47 and 4:32–37. Explain reasons the decision was made. Your explanation might include facts about the life-style of Jesus and those who followed him (see Matt. 9:35–10:10; Mark 10:28–31; Luke 8:1–3; 9:57–62; 10:1–12; 14:7–14; 19:1–10) as well as some of the teachings of Jesus related to what provides real security in life and the role of wealth, property, and possessions in human existence (see Matt. 7:7–11; 20:1–16; 25:31–46; Mark 10:17–31, 35–45; Luke 6:20–36; 12:13–34; 16:1–15, 19–31; 21:1–4; John 10:14–17).

Getting in Touch with Your Experience and Action Needs

Fiorenza (pp. 153–154) presents us with the following challenge and hope:

> As a feminist vision, the *basileia* vision of Jesus calls all women without exception to wholeness and selfhood, as well as to solidarity with those women who are the impoverished, the maimed, and outcasts of society and church. It knows of the deadly violence such a vision and commitment will encounter. It enables us not to despair or to relinquish the struggle in the face of such violence. It empowers us to walk upright, freed from the double oppression of societal and religious sexism and prejudice. The woman-identified man, Jesus, called forth a discipleship of equals that still needs to be discovered and released by women and men today.

1. What does such wholeness and solidarity mean for you? Can you identify relationships or particular groups in which you experience such wholeness and solidarity?

2. Considering the vision of an inclusive, caring, and liberating community, how does your congregation compare with such a vision?

3. Name one initial step you would like to take toward that "discipleship of equals that still needs to be discovered and released."

SECTION 5

Faith and Economics

The material in this section is intended to enable you to write your own statement of theology dealing with economics and the Christian faith.

Reflections on Storytelling and Shared Faith

Sheila Collins, who has worked with the National Division of the Board of Global Ministries of The United Methodist Church, has written about the function the process of collective storytelling had in forming and understanding the Bible. She also explains the role storytelling continues to have as we presently participate in the activity of God in human history. When creating our own theological understanding of contemporary economic realities and in discerning the Spirit and will of Christ in our midst, the process described by Collins can be of great value.

Reclaiming the Bible Through Storytelling

When I attended seminary, theology began deductively, with abstract syllogisms composed by men, usually with German names—men who had never had to change and wash dirty diapers, sit for six hours in the welfare office, stay up all night with a sick child, pick cotton in a dusty field, sell their bodies for a living, or work all day in the mills then come home to do the dinner, the laundry, and the dishes.

Such men had wives and secretaries to take care of their bodily needs. Their sons and daughters went to Harvard and Oberlin (or their German equivalents), not to Pleiku or the Scotia mine pits. They were paid handsomely to spin out beautiful theories which only their peers could understand. They claimed that their theories were derived from the Bible, and it took them hundreds of pages to explain why. . . .

If theology is to be meaningful for us, it must not start with abstractions, but with *our stories*—just as the early Hebrews and Christians of the Bible began with theirs. Somehow, our churches got the order reversed. How many of us were taught as children to memorize Bible stories and verses before we ever understood or had a chance to articulate our own story? We cannot appreciate the meaning of another's experience—especially if that experience occurred two and three thousand years ago—until we have asked the right questions of our own.

I see the Bible, not as a set of facts or propositions to which we must twist experience to fit, but as a guide or primer to participating in the creation of our own biblical history. . . . To the extent that those of us who call ourselves Christian still find important the cluster of meanings surrounding the Exodus, the entry into the Promised Land, the ministry, death, and resurrection of Jesus, we participate in shaping the continuation of that story, just as surely as did Moses and Miriam, Peter, Priscilla, and Paul.

Theology begins with our stories: What we do with our time; how we feel about our children, our husbands, our bosses; how we feel about money and who gets it; . . . what pains us, enrages us, saddens and humiliates us; what makes us laugh; what enlightens and empowers us; what keeps us holding on in moments of despair; where we find separation and alienation; where we find true community and trust.

When I say that theology starts with our stories I am not saying anything new. Testifying is a cherished tradition and telling our stories to one another is what women have always done—over the garden fence, at the food co-op, down at the pump. The tradition is the same; only the structure and significance we give to it are different.

Testifying in church usually signifies you've already been saved. One isn't supposed to talk about troubles unless one's already found Jesus and arrived in the Promised Land. But if you're still in the wilderness, it's pretty hard to see your way through. And if you're still in bondage back in Egypt, you might not even know there is a liberator who has just been found among the bullrushes. Yet if the Hebrews had not preserved the stories as they went along—stories of groaning and complaining; stories of despair—if they had had no rich oral tradition to preserve the sting of the lash, the memory of having sown while another reaped, how would they have known what the taste of liberation was all about? How would they have recognized it when it came? . . .

The Hebrews told their stories as a conscious political act in order to define themselves over against the dominant cultures of their day. The early Christians who preserved the stories of Jesus paid for these political acts with their lives. They told the story of Jesus in such a way as to set him over against the imperial, emperor worshipping cult of Rome. The story was so powerful that Rome had finally to co-opt it in establishing Christianity as a state religion under the emperor Constantine. Women were part of the power of that early story. Perhaps that is why it was so subversive of both established religion and the state. Women were the first to tell the world of the events of the resurrection. They traveled around as preachers and teachers of the new message, refusing to play the tradition-bound roles of breeder and domestic. . . .

In the process of collective storytelling [today] we begin to see patterns; networks of oppression connecting women in Harlan, Kentucky, with women in Altoona, Pennsylvania, and upstate New York. . . . We begin to ask ourselves: Why these patterns of defeat? Why after a century of struggle is our land more devastated than ever; why after the advent of birth control and women's liberation are more thirteen-, fourteen-, and fifteen-year-olds having babies than ever before and why are women in Puerto Rico, New York, on Indian reservations, and in Appalachia being sterilized in large numbers? Why are women, as a group, losing ground according to every socioeconomic indicator available? Recognizing that our oppression is so widespread, our defeats so redundant, relativizes our suffering. We no longer feel ashamed of our failure to live up to the individualized standards set by the men in Washington or on Madison Avenue, knowing that our opposition is a small part of the systematized repression of the majority of the earth's people.

Such knowledge is powerful. We begin to identify not with the privileged, whom we have always been taught to emulate, but with the common people of the earth. It was such identification Jesus talked about in his Sermon on the Mount. A colonialist church has never been able to understand the meaning of those passages which speak of the first being last and the meek inheriting the earth. Such knowledge is the beginning of wisdom. . . .

As we collect our stories, they begin to shape themselves into a body of experience—a kind of litany—which can no longer be denied. They become the means for a collective self-expression which feeds and strengthens those who are able to hear, just as the stories of the Hebrews in bondage in Egypt, in flight and in temporary restitution, repeated generation after generation, have strengthened the diaspora. Just as the stories of Jesus, told and retold, sustained the early Christian community through persecution.

Through the telling and retelling of our stories, the inessentials are gradually sloughed off—those inessentials like varied colors and shapes of leaves—until only the veins, the life-bearing vessels, remain. It is then that we begin to see the patterns of triumph, steadfastness, salvation, and liberation inherent in them. As the early Hebrews

and early Christians looked back over their lives and discovered these patterns, so we discover what it was in women's experience which has kept women going through tragedy and devastation, through the daily rituals of feeding and caring. We discover the secret which keeps hope more alive in the oppressed who are conscious of the source of their oppression than in those who do the oppressing. Only then can we name that which has brought us through as the God of our experience, and distinguish with any clarity the true prophets from the false.

The process of discovering and naming that God is the process of our own liberation or salvation.

As we redefine ourselves through the telling of our stories, discover the sources and patterns of our oppression, and name the God of *our* salvation, we begin to reappropriate the Christian tradition and the special folkways in which it was transmitted in a way which is truly empowering and liberating.

Perhaps when Appalachian women begin to share the stories of how their sons were dragged off to a war in Southeast Asia, fought to propitiate the American male god of power, they can identify with that Sarah of ancient times who watched in the same immobilized way as her husband, Abraham, took the son of her old age to the mountains as an offering, in the mistaken notion that God demands the sacrifice of the innocents for the sins of the guilty.

Perhaps when black women share stories of how their sons and husbands were taken from them through slavery, hunger, dope, war, and the criminal justice system, they can gain strength through remembering Hagar, Abraham's concubine, who through the jealousy of Sarah was banished to the wilderness with her infant son but because of her faithfulness was promised by God that her son would live to establish a nation.

Perhaps when Appalachian women begin to share stories of their aunts who, driven from the farms to the cities during the Depression, ended up as prostitutes—the only job they could get which would pay them enough to send some back home—only then perhaps will we truly identify with the woman of ill-repute, who bathed Jesus' feet with her tears and whose implicit faithfulness has become a part of the record of salvation.

Perhaps when the day comes that black and white women, poor and middle-class women are able to share their stories—and through that sharing to discover the painful contradictions of women's existence in a patriarchal, competitive, and profit-oriented society—then, perhaps, there can be a reconciliation between Sarah the wife and Hagar the concubine.

When we have brought to consciousness, articulated, and honed to the essentials the stories of our bondage and liberation, then we can reconnect with the buried traditions in our own folk history. No people are ever willingly, or without resistance, colonized. We should learn to look for those remnants of resistance which are often disguised as passivity, stubbornness, hostility, and superstition. We can use that wonderful democratic tradition of "testifying" in church to talk about how the coal and textile companies, the family planning experts, and the welfare officials are keeping women down, and how, by participating in that sit-in at the welfare office, we are able to get food in our stomachs and spirit for our souls. We can take all those marvelous hymns which give us the shivers when we sing them and change the words around; changing the "I's" to "we's," the male pronouns to generic ones, the "blood of the Savior" to the blood of our sisters and brothers killed in the mines and the floods, and those mansions in the sky by-and-by to the green rolling hills of West Virginia. We can rediscover the forgotten heroines embedded in our history and name them in our services when it comes time for a recollection of the saints.

Questions for Reflection

1. Why does Collins think it is important for our theology to start with our stories rather than with abstract concepts? What examples can you recall as illustrations of creating theological understandings from your life experiences?

2. How can the Bible be a "guide or primer to participation in the creation of our own biblical history"? In what ways do Christians today "participate in shaping the continuation" of the biblical story?

3. In what ways can storytelling be "a conscious political act" in which we define ourselves over against our dominant culture?

Getting in Touch with Your Own Theological Understandings

1. Look back at your findings from your economic history and from the stories of Gaynell Begley, Min Chong Suk, and Lucia. What sources and patterns of oppression did you identify? What relationships did you see between sexism, racism, and classism in our historical experience? What role does our nation play in the international economic system?

2. Now consider God's liberation of the Hebrews in the Exodus event (Ex. 1–15) and God's liberation of all oppressed persons in Jesus Christ and stories you have told or heard of economic liberation occurring today.

3. Keeping the above in mind, write a letter dealing with the general subject of Faith and Economics. You might model it after the epistles from Paul in the Bible.

A theological statement on Christian Faith and Economic Justice was approved by the 196th (1984) General Assembly of the Presbyterian Church (U.S.A.). It contained the following:

God Does and Demands Justice
Whatever else the God of the Bible is, this One is a God of justice (Is. 30:18). God loves justice (Is. 61:8), delights in justice (Jer. 9:24), executes justice (Ps. 140:12), promises to establish justice (Is. 42:4), and demands justice (Deut. 16:20). Whatever else honoring this God entails, it requires that we hunger and thirst after God's righteousness which includes God's justice (Mt. 5:6), that we seek God's kingdom and God's justice above all else (Mt. 6:33), and that we follow justice and only justice in our common life (Deut. 16:20). The justice God does and expects is one of the Bible's greatest and most pervasive themes.

In the Bible God's justice is not something opposed to God's love but a manifestation of it. The two ideas are closely associated in such passages as these: "The Lord is just in all his ways, and kind in all his doings" (Ps. 145:17). God "executes justice for the fatherless and the widow and loves the sojourner, giving him food and clothing" (Deut. 10:18). Justice is God's love distributed. It is displayed especially in God's deliverance of those in need: ". . . the Lord maintains the cause of the afflicted, and executes justice for the needy" (Ps. 140:12). It is God "who executes justice for the oppressed; who gives food to the hungry" (Ps. 146:5–7).

Although this statement is an abstraction drawn from the story of the Bible, it can be helpful to us in identifying some questions to ask of our life experiences, such as:

1. What in our experience provides knowledge that God loves justice and requires justice in our common lives?

2. What networks of oppression have you identified in your story so far? What makes you think that God is concerned about this oppression?

3. Where and how have you or your sisters experienced God's loving justice? liberation? salvation?

4. What is the source of your hope for a more loving, compassionate, and just society?

5. What other questions that arise out of your life situation or our shared economic life should be addressed in your statement?

Now write your own statement on Faith and Economic Justice, sharing your understandings about God and God's concern and action for justice in the present.

SECTION 6

Assumptions, Values, Beliefs, and Economics

In this section, we will explore some of the basic assumptions, values, and beliefs that undergird and sustain our present economic system and work life. We shall then evaluate these against the biblical shalom vision.

Reflections on Shalom

In preparation for the evaluative process you will be involved in, spend a few minutes reflecting on the shalom (peace) vision. Walter Brueggemann has said of that vision, "The central vision of world history is that all creation is one, every creature in community with every other, living in harmony and security toward the joy and well being of every other creature." Before looking at some passages which communicate this life-changing vision, ponder Brueggemann's statement, seeking to let it explode in your mind and heart. As you will note, *shalom* has a fuller meaning than is denoted by our word *peace*.

Now spend a few minutes relaxing, slowing down the many interrupting thoughts and centering yourself. A simple way to do this is to close your eyes, follow the path of your breathing, and then start counting downward from 50, with each exhalation moving to a lower number and greater depth within yourself. Then read the passages below. Listen with your heart and imagination, letting the words release visual, feeling, or thought images.

The wolf shall dwell with the lamb,
   and the leopard shall lie down with the kid,
and the calf and the lion and the fatling together,
   and a little child shall lead them.
The cow and the bear shall feed;
   their young shall lie down together;
   and the lion shall eat straw like the ox.
The sucking child shall play over the hole of the asp,
   and the weaned child shall put his hand on the
     adder's den.
They shall not hurt or destroy
   in all my holy mountain;
for the earth shall be full of the knowledge of the
   LORD
   as the waters cover the sea.

(Isaiah 11:6–9)

For he [God] has made known to us in all wisdom and insight the mystery of his will, according to his purpose which he set forth in Christ as a plan for the fulness of time, to unite all things in him, things in heaven and things on earth.

(Ephesians 1:9–10)

And he [Christ] came and preached peace to you who were far off and peace to those who were near; for through him we both have access in one Spirit to the Father. So then . . . you are fellow citizens with the saints and members of the household of God, built upon the foundation of the apostles and prophets, Christ Jesus himself being the cornerstone, in whom the whole structure is joined together and grows into a holy temple in the Lord; in whom you also are built into it for a dwelling place of God in the Spirit.

(Ephesians 2:17–22)

Then I saw a new heaven and a new earth; for the first heaven and the first earth had passed away, and the sea was no more. And I saw the holy city, new Jerusalem, coming down out of heaven from God, prepared as a bride adorned for her husband; and I heard a loud voice from the throne saying, "Behold, the dwelling of God is with men. He will dwell with them, and they shall be his people . . . ; he will wipe away every tear from their eyes, and death shall be no more, neither shall there be mourning nor crying nor pain any more, for the former things have passed away.

(Revelation 21:1–4)

Additional passages to reflect on that communicate aspects of the shalom vision are:

Isaiah 9:4–7; 55:1–3, 8–13; 65:17–25
Ezekiel 34:25–31; 37:26–28
Hosea 2:18–22
Luke 1:50–55
Galatians 3:25–29

Before moving on, list some of the basic values which are embodied in the shalom vision.

Entering Into Another's Analysis of Cultural Values

Following are some values, commonly held beliefs, and assumptions that undergird and flow out of our society's materialistic, scientific, and technological world view. These are rarely articulated or acknowledged. These convictions also show the influence of our culture's tendency toward hierarchical thinking (see Section 3).

Faith is placed in "man-made" environments that hail rationality, science, and technology as deliverers of humankind. In a world view with these time and space limitations, domination, mastery, excellence, and control are viewed as key human goals. They have helped achieve what is perceived as a "superior" civilization in the West. Through technology and scientific know-how, humanity will make history "turn out right."

Nature is basically a play toy for human domination, use, and consumption. Nature's resources are provided for the ongoing improvement of the material standard of living for individual and social betterment. Indeed, this kind of improvement process gives life meaning and direction.

Material security and abundance bring a real quality of life in which one grows in freedom (consumer freedom to choose this or that). Enough is never enough.

Social progress, communal life, and individual interest are best served by competitive achievement-oriented behavior, which should be rewarded by material goods, status, and power over others and movement up an economic ladder to success. In this movement it is assumed that the "I win" part of our competitive efforts can be disconnected from the "you lose" part (see Elizabeth Dodson Gray, *Green Paradise Lost,* p. 75).

The natural differences in creation indicate that there is a scale of values inherent in creation. Some things, creatures, human beings, and the like are therefore considered "better" or more important than others. Whenever diversity is observed, it must be evaluated and judged against this culturally defined measuring rod. Some work activities, skills, and abilities (such as rational, managerial, and scientific ones) are judged intrinsically superior and more valuable to society than others (such as manual, artistic, and service-oriented ones). Consequently, persons with those "higher" abilities and training should be given greater responsibility, respect, and power. Indeed, some people and groups can be judged inferior by nature, and therefore their contributions to society need not be valued, remembered, or rewarded as highly as others. Instead, these persons may be judged to have fewer and differing needs from the superior and dominant group.

The most effective and efficient way to arrange society's work activities is to have detailed, sharply defined divisions of role and function in specific places, within a particular time frame and often with a highly developed technical language. For some groups of "lesser persons" with "inferior skills," this means a life of dehumanizing, alienating labor as a mere means of existence.

Questions for Reflection

1. Are these really the values, beliefs, or convictions that undergird our economic and social life? Are there ones you question? Can you think of others that should be added?

2. How has each assumption affected women and racial and ethnic minorities in this country? Which assumptions make inequity and oppression of some sort necessary?

3. How does each assumption affect the international economic scene?

4. How would you evaluate each assumption against values communicated through Jesus' teachings, the biblical vision of shalom, and your own statement about faith and economic justice?

Getting in Touch with Your Own Degree of Acculturation

Read through the assumptions again, exploring ways this "hidden agenda" may have affected your life. Explore the following areas:

1. Your feelings of self-worth, your feelings and thoughts about your primary work activity, your life-style, your goals in life.

2. Your view of competition, independence and dependence, power, control, authority, dominance and submission, etc.

3. Your relationship to persons different from you and/or the dominant culture.

4. Your thoughts and feelings about other nations, especially underdeveloped countries and those with different economic arrangements.

5. Your relationship to nature: how you view and respond to the natural world.

6. Your understanding of the relationship of spiritual reality and our "space-time box."

PART THREE

Generating a New Consciousness

SECTION 7

Peace and Economic Security

The material in this section will help you identify connections between the real costs of military spending and the weapons industry and the needs and struggles of ordinary people, especially the poor and disadvantaged. In addition it will help you to explore what provides real security in human life and to envision new ways of using the earth's resources and human abilities, for reconciliation and development internationally and for programs that meet social needs nationally.

Reflections on World Realities

The bomb the United States dropped on Hiroshima on August 6, 1945, killed or injured 130,000 people. A common nuclear warhead today is one megaton, or 80 times more powerful than the Hiroshima bomb. In 1984, despite test bans and Salt I and II, the U.S.A. and U.S.S.R. possessed over 50,000 nuclear warheads (30,000 U.S. as compared with 20,000 Soviet). These have an explosive power equal to four pounds of TNT for every man, woman, and child on earth. In one half hour, all citizens in the northern hemisphere can be destroyed. Yet over the next decade the two superpowers plan to build over 20,000 more warheads, along with a new "generation" of missiles to deliver them at long range. The Reagan administration is determined to put $1.5 *trillion* into new armaments by 1985 "to defend the American way of life" by being "number one" in military strength. In the election year of 1984, with an unprecedented deficit of close to $200 billion and serious cutbacks in domestic programs, Americans were being asked to fund military programs costing $313.4 billion during 1985—a 13 percent increase over current spending, even after accounting for inflation. If this proposal is approved, the average American household will spend $3,400 in taxes on the military in the coming year. The following figures showing the amount committed to the military are helpful for comparison's sake:

1980: $145.8 billion
1989: $456.4 billion

(Because weapons and military construction projects take several years to build, the budget authorization committed to them in a single year is spent over three or four years.)

For many people, the continuation of such expenditures seems absurd, especially in view of the enormous amount of overkill already available. As an MIT physicist said, "We haven't yet adjusted to the idea that if you kill your enemy, you die too." In a nuclear war, the radioactive fallout from our own weapons exploded in Russia would be carried by the wind to contaminate Americans as well as others. Indeed, the earth's environment could change so drastically that no one can say for sure if *any* life could survive. The United States has started a costly program to study the effects of this so-called "nuclear winter."

Certainly, those of us in the United States need to be aware that for every move we make the Russians will make a countermove. Seven times out of ten, major new U.S. weapons were developed several years ahead of those of the

The Arms Race

Year in Which Superpowers Acquired Weapons

	U.S.	U.S.S.R.
Atomic Bomb	1945	1949
Intercontinental Bomber	1948	1955
Hydrogen Bomb	1954	1955
Intercontinental Ballistic Missile	1958	1957
Satellite in Orbit	1958	1957
Submarine Launched Ballistic Missile	1960	1968
Multiple Warhead	1966	1968
Anti-Ballistic Missile	1968	1972
Multiple Independently-Targetable Warhead	1970	1975
Long Range Cruise Missile	1982	?
Neutron Bomb	1983	?

Source: World Military and Social Expenditures

U.S.S.R. (see chart, The Arms Race). We are now in the process of developing new weapons like the cruise missiles. With such weapons in place, the Russians will not want a freeze, feeling once again that they must try to catch up before stopping the arms race. And yet, as Clarence Jordan observed years ago, "Somehow or other, we shrink with horror from the prospect not of annihilation, but of reconciliation."

In 1979 Senator Mark Hatfield proposed a freeze as an amendment to the Salt II Treaty. The Soviet Union has also proposed a freeze, initially on September 28, 1976, at the U.N. It has made similar proposals every year since then.

Even so, the U.S. and the U.S.S.R. are about to start on a new round of the arms race. The new weapons are faster, more accurate, and in some cases smaller (which makes them easier to hide) than present weapons. In the United States, accelerated funding for space-based ballistic missile defense is now a major administrative priority which will carry the arms race into space. "Star wars" become a live option. The result of these new arms will be a hair trigger on the balance of terror that has "kept the peace" between the two superpowers. With both sides jittery, there will be less stability and more chance of the ultimate nuclear holocaust. The new weapons are known as "counter force" or *first-strike* weapons. They are designed not just to deter, but also to fight a nuclear war, making such a war more thinkable.

On May 27–29, 1984, the *Washington Post* carried a three-part article entitled "Thinking the Unthinkable" by *Post* staff writer Rick Atkinson. In the article, Atkinson describes how the Defense Nuclear Agency is trying to "take a peek at what World War III might be like, from outer space to the ocean's depth." Housed in northern Virginia, the agency serves as a kind of "nuclear vicar to the Pentagon." Speaking of the work of DNA, Atkinson states, "It's a strange world—some say a Strangelovian— where model submarines are blasted in the New Mexico desert and MX missiles are fired in Armageddon chambers tucked in a bunker among the three-bedroom split-levels of suburban Maryland. It's a world of sober animal experiments." (Although rats and beagles are also used, one experiment had rhesus monkeys strapped into aircraft trainers, where they were irradiated with various doses of gamma rays to see how long they could guide their trainers with the dosages. Those given the heaviest doses were stricken with violent vomiting, fol-lowed by an extreme degree of lethargy, "leading the Air Force to conclude in 1981 documents that 'satisfactory mission completion . . . would not seem possible for all crew members.'" The monkeys were later put to death.

In what one critic called the "sleaziest job in the Pentagon," a cadre of military scientists and strategists spend most waking hours mulling over the best way to fight World War III. The defense department "argues that thinking the unthinkable is a grim but sensible necessity in a world fraught with nuclear peril, [but] skeptics assert that by building confidence in U.S. nuclear war-fighting prowess, the Pentagon lowers the anxiety threshold and makes doomsday more thinkable."

William M. Arkin, a researcher of the Institute for Policy Studies and one of the authors of the *Nuclear Weapons Databook*, says, "I think the intent of their tests is to prove that nuclear war is controllable and that they can model and mitigate any negative aspects. . . . It's like nuclear narcotics, making you feel you've got everything under control."

Atkinson asserts that "DNA's testing is in search not only of a better defense but also a more lethal offense—in some respects, a better nuclear mouse trap."

Because of space limitations, nothing has been said here about chemical warfare, about the fact that the U.S. and the U.S.S.R. are the major producers and exporters of arms for the world, or about our military solutions to economic problems, especially in Central America.

Countless organizations and individuals find it difficult to understand the endless escalating nuclear arms race, which drains needed resources from meeting human need. Over half our national budget is spent for military expenditures and past wars at a time when two thirds of the world goes to bed hungry. Every minute thirty children die for lack of food or medicine. Within that same minute, the nations of the world spend $1.3 million on their military forces. And this is done while the standard of living is actually declining in most areas of the world.

Within our own country, unemployment rates during the past several years have been between 8 and 10 percent. In March of 1984, a drop to a rate of 7.8 percent was hailed as a triumph when previously economists thought anything over a 4 percent rate was "unacceptable." Now we seem to have accepted the 8 percent level. Yet even this figure is misleading, because it does not count the thousands who have given up looking for work or the large part of the labor force who can find only temporary work. It also doesn't present an accurate picture since among those hardest hit the figures are much higher. At the same time that so many among minorities and women are unable to find jobs, almost all our human services have been pared drastically. Additionally, by placing more resources into military expenditures, which provide fewer jobs than any other areas of the economy, we have actually eliminated job possibilities. A study, "Structure of the U.S. Department of Labor 1980–85," found that $1 billion spent on the military provides an average of 20,000 fewer jobs than the same amount spent in most other areas. Even with this information available, we are not only asked to support escalating arms expenditures, we also are informed that we must continue cutting funds to provide health care for the elderly and needy, aid to dependent children, job training for the unemployed, and perhaps even Social Security.

Entering Into the Hopes of Other Women

Reflect again on Helvi Sipila's statement:

Which is the new force necessary to create a new faith and confidence among people and nations, and to direct the human and material resources into constructive purposes, instead of destructive? . . .

We see the influence of life-creating, life-sustaining values—as contrasted with militaristic aggression, dominance, control, and destructive behaviors that produce "non-products" and "non-services"—reflected in the three major objectives selected by the 1975 United Nations International Women's Year Conference held in Mexico City. At that conference, a world action plan was adopted and the Decade for Women, 1976–1985, was established by the UN to intensify progress toward three objectives: equality for women and men; development, especially in response to the needs of women and with their participation; and world peace.

Clearly, realization of these goals still seems far away. As we have seen, national and international expenditures of money, time, and human and natural resources consistently go toward more traditional sources of "security."

Patricia Mische of Global Education Associates has suggested how to move toward the objectives of the World Plan of Action.

1. *Enlarge our vision and analysis.* We must place our issues in the macro-context of global interdependence and identify all the forces that impinge on our issues. . . .

2. *Work for world order alternatives.* While continuing to press for realization of greater equality and development—the first two goals of the Decade for Women—we must give ever more energy and attention to the third objective, that of peace. In fact it may well be that the order of the three goals should be revised to read *peace,* development and equality. Equality may be the fruit of the first two.

Women, who have been so deeply affected by the subordination of their social worth and needs . . . have an important contribution to make in helping redefine what constitutes *true* world security and *true* national security. They know their personal interests and those of their children can best be assured when a nation's security is measured by the degree to which all its citizens, including women and children, are affirmed as of equal worth. Women know that a nation, like a family, is more truly secure when its basic needs are given priority over balance-of-power struggles. They know true national security will be realized when their children are ensured a world in which they need not fear annihilation or dehumanization.

3. *Be pragmatic and ready for long-range work.* In working for peace we must not only denounce militaristic and other violent approaches to national security. We must do more than remain one step behind the latest development in destructive weaponry or the newest "advance" in arms technology. We must do more than denounce. We must be ready to extend our historic nurturing role to foster the growth of a new era in the human community. We must be ready to work for systems change that can produce constructive alternatives and prevent arms buildup and militarism in the first place.

A Time for Reflection

Read "Balancing the Budget on the Backs of Women" and "Do You Know What Your Tax Dollar Buys?" As you study this material, be aware of how it makes you *feel.* What do you want to do about what you feel?

Economic Conversion

One of the major factors behind the statements you have read is what some people term "our permanent war economy" or "our military/

industrial complex." What they mean is that in reality much of our industry and consequently many workers and communities are dependent on war-related work activities. There are hopeful signs that with the growing momentum of peace efforts domestically and globally, numerous individuals and groups are beginning to think of economic conversion. Such conversion of the economy to productive and peaceful purposes is a crucial factor in shifting political support away from militarism. At present, countless investors, workers at all levels, and communities throughout the world are dependent on arms production and defense-related industries. Economic conversion is a major essential component of movement toward peace. It would include (1) bringing government, management, and workers together to plan alternative uses of military industries before plants closed and (2) planning for income and retraining for workers negatively affected by conversion and layoffs.

Economic conversion is not just dreaming the impossible dream. There is a renewal of interest in conversion. In 1984, Congressman Ted Weiss (D-NY) has reintroduced his Defense Economic Adjustment Act (HR 425), a blueprint for a national conversion policy that would provide federal assistance for planning and implementing conversion on the local level. Also, Representative Nicholas Mavroules (D-MA) has introduced a more limited approach in the Economic Conversion Act (HR 4805), a bill designed to provide income assistance and job training grants to workers and communities affected by major contract cancellations.

In addition, it is hopeful to note that many union members who have generally been perceived as hawkish are making a shift toward peace. Many national labor organizations have endorsed proposals for a bilateral U.S.-Soviet freeze on the testing, production, and deployment of nuclear weapons. Some have been involved in campaigns to stop the MX. Some support nonintervention in Central America. Even though the official AFL-CIO position supports increased military spending, a significant opposition is building up within the membership:

> The Reagan Administration has cut the social welfare "safety net" to shreds. But the billions "saved" have not been returned to the taxpayer. Instead Reagan has shifted them to a ballooning military budget that has nearly doubled since he took office. And there's more to come.
>
> (*Service Employee,* February 1984)

There is also ferment within some labor organizations for developing alternative production possibilities: that is, planning how socially useful products could be made using the same plant, equipment, skills, and tools.

BALANCING THE BUDGET ON THE BACKS OF WOMEN

A balanced budget has been the Reagan Administration's prescription for curing the ills of the economy, although this goal has proven elusive in the face of massive tax cuts for the wealthy and for corporations, which decrease government revenue. Nevertheless, Reagan is committed to spending at least $1.6 trillion on the military in the next five years and at the same time keeping a lid on overall government spending.

So who is bearing the brunt of this balancing act?

It is the poor (those people living below the government-defined poverty level of $9,900 a year for a family of four) and the disadvantaged . . . and that means women. Female-headed households represent 15% of all families, but over half of all poor families. Seventy percent of the female-headed households live in poverty. If the current rate of female-headed households continues to grow, women and their children will compose virtually all of the nation's poor by the year 2000. Women 65 and over are the poorest of the poor, 72% living on $4,359 or less a year.

Minority women, because of the combined effects of racial and sexual discrimination, form a disproportionate share of the poor. Two thirds of all poor Black families are headed by women. Almost half of all families headed by Black and Hispanic women live in poverty. The unemployment rate for Black women is over 18% and over 15% for Hispanic women, compared to 9% for white women.

The number of working women who are poor or "near poor" is large and growing. Three out of five full-time working women earn less than $10,000 a year, one of three earns under $7,000 a year. Women are struggling.

Women are struggling to survive. What little government assistance they once received has been reduced or eliminated. But the federal budget is still not balanced; in fact, the 1984 federal budget [had] the largest deficit ever!

The cause of that deficit is not social programs, it is the military budget, which is the largest "peacetime" budget in our nation's history . . . $274.1 billion for 1984.

Is this how we want our money to be spent?

Reagan Proposed Budget Cuts	*Reagan Proposed Military Spending*

AFDC: Aid to Families with Dependent Children provides direct cash assistance to needy families with children if one parent is dead, absent, or incapacitated. Families in dire poverty qualify for these benefits.

Effects: 3.5 million families receive AFDC; 94% of heads of households of AFDC families are women; 44% of AFDC families are Black.

$1.4 billion on the Trident II missile program.
$6.6 billion on the MX missile program.

Cuts: Reduce funding for 1.2 billion in federal and state funding ($800 million in federal funds). Eligibility and needs requirements were changed, cutting *thousands* of women from the rolls. Over 400,000 people were cut from the rolls in 1982 and 280,000 people received reduced payments.

Proposed Funding: $75 billion for AFDC and Community Service Employment Program (fiscal year 1984).

MEDICAID: Subsidizes medical care to mothers and children, pays one half of all nursing home bills, and assists in long-term care of the elderly.

Effects: 12.8 million of the 22 million recipients of Medicaid are women. 47% of recipients are Black.
Cuts: Reduced funding by $300 million.
Proposed Funding: $20.8 billion.

A $33.6 billion increase in military spending, 14% higher than 1983 levels.
$455 million for the Pershing II missiles.

HOUSING: Provides funds for subsidized housing.

Effects: 40.5% of all subsidized housing units are occupied by the elderly. Three fourths of these units are maintained by women.

$6.9 billion on the B-1B bomber.
$825 million for the Ground Launched Cruise missile.

Cuts: Reduced funding by $7.9 billion since President Reagan took office in 1980. 98% of all federal housing funds have been cut. This year approximately 40,000 public units will be cancelled and 17,600 section 8 units will be cut.
Proposed Funding: $750 million.

FOOD STAMPS: Provides assistance to low-income families for basic food commodities.

Effects: Women and children make up 85% of the food stamp recipients.

$1.4 billion on the AH-64 Army Attack Helicopter.
More than $11 billion on 302 new conventional aircraft.

Cuts: $1.4 billion. One million people were cut from food stamp rolls in 1983.
Proposed Funding: $11.1 billion.

JOB TRAINING PARTNERSHIP ACT: JTPA will only train workers. The President estimates over 1.5 million adults and youths will be trained. Over 600,000 job positions and tens of thousands more training slots had been created by CETA; funding for all those positions has been eliminated.

Effects: At least 50% of all CETA jobs were filled by women and 51.5% by minorities—Title IID and Title VI. Close to one million women are officially "unemployed."

$2.4 million for civil defense programs.
$3.7 billion for 3 CG-47 AEGIS Naval Cruisers.

Cuts: Reduced funding by $121 million at the height of the CETA program (1979), $9 billion was appropriated for employment and training.
Proposed Funding: $3.6 billion.

DO YOU KNOW WHAT YOUR TAX DOLLAR BUYS?

You work hard for your money. But over half of your income taxes pay for the military—53% in 1984.

The Administration's Budget

The Administration claims that the federal government spends more on human resources than on the military. But the true budget picture is hidden by the government's accounting methods. Many military-related costs, including the continuing costs of past wars, are kept in separate categories. And the overall budget is made to seem larger than it really is by lumping together revenue from income taxes with revenue from trust funds, such as Social Security.

These trust funds were set up years ago to provide specific benefits. They are financed by separate taxes. For example, you pay Social Security taxes now and receive benefits when you retire. The federal government merely acts as caretaker for these funds. Neither Congress nor the President can spend the money in the trust funds, except for earmarked purposes. Therefore, if you want to know what happens to your tax dollars which the federal government can spend, the trust funds should be considered as separate cookie jars, not as part of the federal pie.

In fiscal year 1984, total federal outlays (after subtracting trust funds) were $629 billion.

Military: Current military, 39%, includes Defense and Energy departments, nuclear warhead programs, civil defense, military aid, and portions of the NASA and Coast Guard budgets; cost of past wars, 14%, includes veterans' benefits and 60% of the interest on the national debt; total, 53%.

Human Resources—most domestic programs not funded through trust funds: education, training, employment, social services, health, income security, agriculture, community and regional development, natural resources, transportation, environment, and energy—33%.

All other—international affairs, justice, space, general government, and remaining interest on the national debt—14%.

Are You More Secure?

At the end of World War II, no enemy could attack the United States. Today in a nuclear war, the U.S. could be wiped out in less than an hour. The U.S. and the Soviet Union now threaten each other with many thousands of incredibly destructive nuclear weapons.

Are you more secure knowing we can "overkill" the Soviets more times than they can "overkill" us? Are you more secure knowing that U.S. troops and weapons are stationed throughout the world? Are you more secure knowing that the needs of the American people are being neglected while you pay for more dangerous, sophisticated, and expensive weapons? Are you more likely to be threatened by Soviet missiles or by unemployment, a polluted environment, crumbling highways, and skyrocketing federal deficits?

What Can You Do About It?

1. Congress holds the purse strings. Let your Representative and Senators know how you think the federal government should spend your tax dollars.

2. Keep telling him or her. No single letter, phone call, or visit will influence legislation. Get your friends and neighbors to help you maintain a continuing dialogue with your elected representatives.

3. Use this information in letters to the editor, radio call-in shows, and other community forums.

4. Distribute copies of this information at shopping centers, town meetings, unemployment lines, and post offices at tax time.

5. Organize press conferences around spare parts overpricing and other wasteful Pentagon spending practices.

What Can Your Money Buy?

The Reagan Administration's proposed budget
for fiscal year 1985 will increase the military's share to 55%.
Do you know what your money could buy instead?

For the Pentagon	From the People
MX Missile, $5 billion	Child nutrition and food stamps, $3.9 billion
Trident II Missile, $2.3 billion	Employment & training programs, $2.1 billion
M-1 tank, $1.9 billion	Guaranteed student loans, $1.8 billion
Ground-launched Cruise Missile, $0.8 billion	Mass transit, $0.8 billion
Antisatellite and chemical weapons, $350 million	Solar energy research, $385 million

Getting in Touch
with a New Society
Grounded in a New Security

The following exercise in hope may seem highly unrealistic at this time, yet often it is only through using our imagination that we are freed from the sense of powerlessness we experience in our present limited and limiting world view. Life does not have to continue as it has in the past. As Buckminster Fuller has said, "We've now learned enough of the principles to really carry on in a new, completer, or grown-up way with the universe. And stop forever the idea of making human beings struggle to see which is the fittest to survive." One way of moving out of the deadness and hopelessness we often feel when we limit ourselves to what seems possible within the present world order is to envision new worlds and dream new dreams. Visions not only provide a way of evaluating present systems and structures, they can also serve as a guide for movement toward fundamental change. Without them we cannot become agents of transformation in our world.

An Exercise in Hope

Our government has just decided to dismantle its military production and activities. This not only means that there will be almost twice as much money in the federal budget for all other expenditures, it also means that between 30 and 50 percent of our nation's top engineers and scientists and all military personnel can be moved from defense to civilian industries and services. In addition, industrial facilities, airports, camps, and the like can be converted for peacetime activities, and natural resources used presently for military hardware can be used to meet public needs. Keep in mind the number of new jobs that can be created to lower unemployment, because money invested in service and other areas provides more jobs.

After quickly identifying root sources of tension in today's world, your task is to brainstorm what you will do with the capital, human time, energy and expertise, military facilities, and natural resources that are now available as a result of the government's decision.

1. As a global citizen, how will you use them to promote reconciliation, peace, development, and equality internationally? What new kind of security will come into existence with your transformations?
2. As a citizen of the United States, how will you use these resources locally to meet human needs and to promote equality and a more human style of life for all?

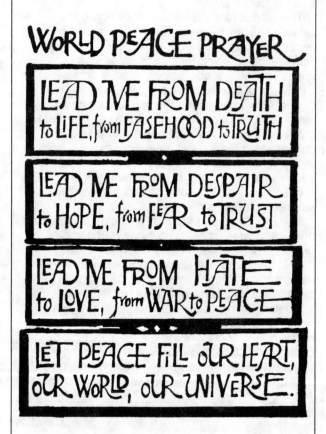

WORLD PEACE PRAYER

LEAD ME FROM DEATH to LIFE, from FALSEHOOD to TRUTH

LEAD ME FROM DESPAIR to HOPE, from FEAR to TRUST

LEAD ME FROM HATE to LOVE, from WAR to PEACE

LET PEACE FILL OUR HEART, OUR WORLD, OUR UNIVERSE.

SECTION 8

From Dreams and Visions to Reality

In this section you will be using your critique of present economic arrangements, the biblical vision of peace, unity, and justice, and your own hopes, dreams, and visions to create an economic model that might reflect more caring and just ways of relating to other persons and God's total creation.

Reflections on Envisioning

As in the last section, you will be asked to exercise your imagination. Frequently because of our scientific "this world" orientation, we may associate the products of our imagination with the illusory, the unreal, even the false. We often underestimate the power of the imagination not only to create new ideas but also to bring into existence that which is radically new. According to Linda Clark and others (p. 3),

> The imagination is a property of mind that, functioning below the level of intellect, converts what are purely sense experiences into images. Imagination is thought prior to the thinking of the intellect, the process that people usually associate with the total activity of the mind. Out of sensation and feeling, the mind creates mental images that provide the basis for more abstract functioning of the intellect.

In addition, the part of the mind that Jung termed the collective unconscious can be freed to feed the imagination with a wealth of inherited wisdom and insight that the individual shares with all humankind. According to Scott Peck, who at one point identifies the unconscious with God, the unconscious is always ahead of the conscious mind, urging growth toward full maturity. Thus the images of the imagination "provide new material for the intellect which brings it into relationship with the old, shaping the new, more comprehensive perceptions of reality. . . . The images may be highly personal . . . or they may illuminate experience in such a way that they become a kind of revelation of the meaning of human life itself" (Ibid., p. 4). In this sense, imagination becomes a source of inspiration above the threshold of ordinary consciousness, frequently releasing the patterns of interconnected life that are inherent within the universe. Consequently, dreaming new dreams and envisioning alternative worlds and structures for relating is one of the critical tasks needed if we are to create more humane and fulfilling work arrangements and economic structures that are directed toward greater justice, equity, and support for all. Of course, the new images are not complete until they begin to take shape in the physical realm, but without them there is no hope. As Richard Shaull says (p. 140), "We die when we settle for the limited possibilities of a dying order (our present world structure) . . . we come alive and become agents of transformation when we begin to live now the as-yet unrealized possibilities around us, whose time has come."

Think for a moment. What persons do you recall whose hopes and visions brought and are still bringing new realities into existence? What about Elizabeth Cady Stanton's dream that women should have the right to vote? Or the dream of Martin Luther King, Jr., that all God's people be able to join hands and sing, "Free at last, free at last, Thank God a'mighty, I'm free at last."

Certainly much of the Bible communicates hopes and visions which as yet are only partially realized. Let us enter into one of those hope-filled images included in Paul's letter to the Corinthians, a disorderly and faction-split community of people who evidently thought some spiritual gifts were more important than others. Reflecting on this problem, Paul rises to "see" something of the full nature of the church, a living organism similar to the physical body. This image is exceedingly fruitful and suggestive. Following Paul's intended meaning, we generally read this passage in terms of the individual's relationship to others in a community or the relationship of a congregation or denomination to the total body of Christ. However, with our present understanding of the interconnectedness and interdependence of all people—and, indeed, all that is—we can expand this vision to gain knowledge of new arrangements for living that reflect the deep wisdom contained in this vision of an organic whole. This wholeness arises out of interrelated variety, difference, and multiplicity. Beneath this vision is the interconnected wholeness in which every bit of being participates.

Before turning to Paul's image in 1 Corinthians 12:4–13:13, center and relax yourself so that you can let go of everyday concerns and move into that deeper level of experience where new dreams are generated and hope and faith are fed. Simply sit or lie down in a comfortable position. Follow your breathing and with each inhalation draw in God-given energy, remembering that for the Hebrews to breathe was to draw in the Spirit of God. With each exhalation, gently say the word *peace*, visualizing all stress, tension, and discord flowing out of your body and mind. Continue following your breathing. After a few minutes, as you sense your body settling down and your consciousness moving to deeper levels, turn to Paul's words. Let them speak to you about the gifts that different peoples, nations, cultures, societies, and races bring to the global community.

Allow Paul's words to call forth their own images, hopes, or related visions and dreams. Be aware that God can and does speak to us, so meditate on the words slowly and expectantly.

Other passages related to the unity of God's creation and God's plan for Shalom that could be pondered in the same manner are Psalm 104, (a magnificent statement of the interdependence of creation; you might enjoy writing a similar psalm from a contemporary world view); Isaiah 2:2–5; Colossians 1:5–20; 3:11–15; John 10:15–16; 2 Corinthians 5:16–21; 8:13–14; Revelation 21:1–6.

Jot down insights from your journey into visions.

Questions for Reflection

1. What patterns of interrelationships do you see?
2. What welds the whole together in one common world?

Entering Into the Vision of Other Women

Remember Helvi Sipila's statement that women "could become the new, dynamic force to create change, change in the minds, attitudes, behavior, and action of all people." A significant reason this is true is that only now are we beginning to listen to, understand, and value women's experience. As Carol Gilligan says (pp. 62–63, 173, 174), this reveals a different mode of social experience and interpretation from men.

In the different voice of women lies the truth of an ethic of care, the tie between relationship and responsibility, and the origins of aggression in the failure of connection. . . .

The reinterpretation of women's experience in terms of their own imagery of relationships . . . provides a nonhierarchical vision of human connection. Since relationships, when cast in the image of hierarchy [the male ladder model], appear inherently unstable and morally problematic, their transposition into the image of web [female model] changes an order of inequality into a structure of interconnection. . . . The experiences of inequality and interconnection, inherent in the relation of parent and child, then gives rise to the ethics of justice and care, the ideals of human relationship—the vision that self and other will be treated as of equal worth, that despite differences in power, things will be fair; the vision that everyone will be responded to and included, that no one will be left alone or hurt. . . . While an ethic of justice proceeds from the premise of equality . . . an ethic of care rests on the premise of nonviolence. . . . In the representation of maturity, both perspectives converge in the realization that just as inequity adversely affects both partners in an unequal relationship, so too violence is destructive for everyone involved. This dialogue between fairness and care not only provides a better understanding of relations between the sexes but also gives rise to a more comprehensive portrayal of adult work and family relationships [and, we might add, social arrangements] . . . and a more generative view of human life.

Here is a vision that flows from women's experience:

A Cooperative Model

Women seek a reconstruction of relationships for which we have neither words nor models; a reconstruction which can give each person the fullness of their being stolen from them by false polarizations (male/female, soul/body, consciousness/nature, material/spiritual, sacred/secular, this world/the next, etc.) . . . and we must seek the fundamental reconstruction of the way resources are allocated within the world community. This implies a reconstruction of our basic models of interrelationships between persons, social groups, and, finally, between human beings and nature. Our model of relationships must cease to be hierarchical and become mutually supportive—a cooperative model of the fellowship of life systems.

(Rosemary Radford Ruether, *New Woman, New Earth*)

Getting in Touch with Your Own Dreams and Visions

Center yourself, using a process similar to that suggested in Section 1. Read through the following fantasy several times before actually engaging your imagination. Then, as you enter into the fantasy, allow your images to flow freely, placing no limits or "realistic" restrictions on them.

With your eyes closed, envision what you would like your life to be like. Imagine what for you would be a blessed life. Begin by seeing yourself waking up one weekday morning five years from today. As you slowly awaken, move gently through the day that is ahead of you, from rising to bedtime. What will you be reading in the newspaper? What kind of activities will you be involved in? Who will you be living, working, and playing with? Who will benefit from these activities? How will the activities be carried out? Which of your own needs will be met by those activities? What is of utmost importance to you? What life-style will be reflected in your day? What kind of technology will you use? Where will you be living? What will you wear and eat?

After your fantasy, list the values reflected in it. For example, if you saw yourself skipping through a grassy field with a flock of children, your fantasy may reflect a high value placed on nurturing, pastoral life, and play activities.

Having fantasized a blessed life, now envision new economic arrangements. See yourself as an economic adviser who has been given the task of creating an economic system from scratch for a community of 100,000 persons. It is assumed that this community has reasonable though not unlimited material resources and abilities and skills. Do not assume that as economic adviser you will have a position of authority or power in the society. Rather, you do not know what place you will have in these new arrangements. The task is to create new economic arrangements in broad outline, not specific social structures. Remember, the fundamental questions of economics are:

1. How shall property, resources, wealth, and the means of production be controlled and distributed?

2. Who shall produce or do what for whom?

Using the Work Sheet for Creating a New Society, write down your vision. After you have thought through the work sheet, you might draw a picture or diagram to sharpen your vision's meaning.

Work Sheet for Creating a New Society

Your task is to create a new society that will be more just, sustainable, and participatory. You can establish for this society any economic arrangement you choose. Your arrangements should care for and be fair to every member of this society.

Make these assumptions:

Your society is a community of 100,000 people.
Your society has access to a reasonable though not unlimited amount of material resources and has, or can have, a reasonable number of farms, factories, and shops.
Many members of your society are potentially productive workers, but they have different skills and talents.
Some members of your society—the very young, the very old, the infirm and disabled—have very limited or no capacity to produce.
"For all have sinned and fall short of the glory of God."

Use the questions that follow to help think through what concerns you need to address as you fashion a new society.

1. *Regarding ownership and distribution:* How will property, resources, and means of production be controlled and distributed? Who will make these decisions?

2. *Regarding goods, services, and technology:* Who will decide what products and services are needed? What level of technology will be needed so that basic needs are met and natural resources are conserved? Who will make these decisions?

3. *Regarding work:* How will it be determined who does what work in your society? For example, how will it be determined who will clean the toilet bowls and do other less exciting but socially needed work? Will there be a sharp division of labor with narrow roles and functions? Can you plan to use the varied abilities and talents of all your members? Can work activities be shared so that each individual has the ability to develop his or her own potentials? Who will be trained for what? How will these decisions be made?

4. *Regarding compensation:* Will everyone in your society receive equal compensation? If not, how will you justify inequalities? On what grounds will it be determined who gets what income?

1. Reflecting on your creation, what basic changes or transformations do you see being called for in our present society?

2. What steps could you take now to begin working on those changes?

PART FOUR

Initiating a Change Process

SECTION 9

Looking Back, Looking Forward

In the material that follows, we will turn back from visions and dreams to look at some hard realities and frightening trends for women in the United States. We shall then look forward to some new factors that offer hope for reversing these trends.

Reflections on Present Trends

There is an alarming development in the economic life of the United States. As you read on, try to analyze and list root causes that may be promoting this tendency in our economy.

The Feminization of Poverty

During the mid-sixties and until the mid-seventies, the number of poor adult males declined while the number of poor females who were heads of households grew by 100,000 yearly. In 1978, sociologist Diana Pearce labeled this trend the "feminization of poverty." By 1982, Barbara Ehrenreich and Karin Stallard were writing in the July–August Ms. *magazine that "if the phrase is not yet a household expression, it may be because public officials are loath to advertise the fact that the prime victims of service cutbacks are women—women and their dependent children. . . . The feminization of poverty—or, to put it the other way, the impoverishment of women—may be the most crucial challenge facing feminism today." The article that follows, by Barbara Ehrenreich and Frances Fox Piven, examines this challenge.*

To judge from the Democratic response to years of budget cuts, traditional New Deal liberation has gone the way of chivalry. While the Reagan administration savaged social programs that serve primarily women and children, most congressional Democrats protested only feebly. Neoliberals, like Senators Paul Tsongas and Gary Hart, actually joined in the call for "belt-tightening."

But where mainstream Democrats fear to tread, feminism is moving in. At the national level, in California and scattered other locations, coalitions of women's groups are organizing to protest social spending cuts and to defend America's embattled welfare state. If the emerging feminist advocacy for the poor gains momentum and resolve, it could be one of the most important factors in the political calculus of the '80s. . . .

What is behind this most recent phase of feminist advocacy for the poor is a development that became apparent only in the late '70s: the feminization of poverty. The poor, who have long been disproportionately black and Hispanic, are now also disproportionately female, and as sociologist Diana Pearce emphasizes, the relative impoverishment of women has occurred in all racial groups. By 1980, two out of three adults whose incomes fell below the official poverty line were women, and more than half the poor families in the nation were headed by women. Observing the trend, the National Advisory Council on Economic Opportunity (since disbanded by the Reagan administration) announced in 1981: "All other things being equal, if the proportion of the poor in female-householder families were to continue to increase at the same rate as it did from 1967 to 1978, the poverty population would be composed solely of women and their children before the year 2000."

In part because of the feminization of poverty, women are much more likely than men to be dependent on government social welfare programs. More than one third of our nation's female-headed families receive AFDC (our principal form of welfare), and they account for 78.9 percent of the families on AFDC. Female-headed households also predominate among the recipients of food stamps, Medicaid, fuel aid assistance, subsidized housing, and supplemental nutritional programs for infants and pregnant women. In addition, women's greater longevity means that women are disproportionately represented among the beneficiaries of Medicare and Social Security.

These programs have been critical to the survival of the poor and the elderly, but even before Reagan's cutbacks, they fell far short of providing a decent standard of living. The average monthly payment on AFDC was slightly under $300 a month for a family of three in 1980, and in no state was (or is) the combination of food stamps and AFDC enough to lift a family *up to* the poverty level.

The number of women who are poor or near-poor, and hence potentially dependent on social welfare programs, is only likely to keep increasing, whether or not the much-heralded economic upturn takes off. One reason is that marriage no longer offers lifelong economic security, even to women in the middle to upper-middle classes. One out of two marriages ends in divorce, and after the breakups, 80 percent of the children remain with their mothers. Whether due to women getting divorced, being widowed, or simply never having married, there are now 9.4 million families headed by women, and the number of these families is increasing several times faster than the number of traditional, male-headed families. (46.8 percent of black families are now female-headed, compared to 13.4 percent of white families, but female-headed families are now increasing more rapidly among whites than blacks.) For most female-headed families, the absent male is a negligible source of income; alimony is a privilege reserved for the ex-wives of millionaires, and child-support payments average less than $2,000 a year when they are paid at all.

Most women, single or married, have entered the job market, but here, too, the financial prospects are bleak. Women are, as they have been since the dawn of industrial capitalism, "cheap labor," today earning only 60 percent of what men do, for a median annual income of $11,591. (The federally defined poverty level is now $8,220 for a family of three.) Most employed women occupy low-paid, dead-end, stereotypically women's jobs— and have little possibility of escaping to anything better. In fact, the amount of low-paid "women's work" is increasing, largely because of the long-term shift away from heavy manufacturing (which has been highly unionized and relatively well paid) and toward service and clerical jobs. According to Emma Rothschild, 70 percent of all new private-sector jobs created between 1973 and 1980 were stereotypically female jobs in such areas as data processing, health care, and, significantly, fast foods. So the time-honored solution to male poverty—more jobs—does not help. A woman can work full time, year round, and still remain poor. . . .

The feminization of poverty—or, more accurately, the impoverishment of women—is mobilizing the broadest spectrum of women's groups since the Equal Rights Amendment countdown. From the left wing of feminism all the way to such staid groups as the League of Women Voters and the American Association of University Women, women are organizing conferences and public hearings, issuing reports, and lobbying with a high level of energy and unity. But when it comes to developing solutions, there is, it seems to us, a curious hesitancy. Most of the agitation around women's poverty has been more reactive than visionary and all too narrowly focused on Reagan's budget cuts—as if the solution lay in a restoration of the Carter era plus, perhaps, the apprehension of child-support defaulters. Even in the protests against the cuts, there is a reluctance to counter the conservative ideology that justifies them. No one seems willing to assert the old liberal (and feminist) conviction that government, if it is to have any moral credibility, *must* take responsibility for the economic security of its citizens, and especially for those—like women, minorities, the elderly—who are severely disadvantaged in the labor market. No one seems willing to go beyond protesting the

cuts to demanding a vast *expansion* of income supports and social services.

Yet for the millions of women who are poor or who risk falling into poverty, there is little alternative. Jobs, at least the kind being generated by the private sector, are not the solution; they are part of the problem. It's hard, too, to organize for better pay when there is no real social "safety net" outside, and getting fired could mean destitution for oneself and one's children. Even if much-better-paying jobs were to proliferate (thanks to some unlikely high-tech miracle), they would be inaccessible to many women in the absence of quality child care, subsidized training programs, and a range of other services. . . .

The political defense of social welfare programs [is] easier if we simultaneously fight for their expansion and reform. For one thing, the present arbitrary fragmentation of programs keeps the potential constituency for social spending divided; we have Medicaid and Medicare instead of a universal system of national health insurance; AFDC and unemployment compensation instead of a single system of income supports; and the beneficiaries of one program come to feel they have little in common with the beneficiaries of another. We need to work for the consolidation of social welfare programs in ways that make administrative sense (like *one* system of health insurance) and unite beneficiaries across lines of class, race, and sex. At the same time, of course, we need to fight for *better* programs even while we fight to preserve the limited programs we have. No one can get too excited about cuts in programs that are niggardly in their benefits and insulting to their beneficiaries. But good programs, programs that enhance individual and community pride, would not be as vulnerable. . . .

One of the most enduring elements of the feminist vision is that of the ultimate triumph of "feminine values"—of caring, compassion, and nurturance—in the sphere of public life. This is the vision that unites our generation with the more conservative feminists of the late nineteenth century; we do not want "maternal values" and virtues to be perpetually marginalized to us or to our homes. We want caring to prevail; we want nurturance to be an organizing principle of our society.

In their article in *Ms.* quoted earlier, Stallard and Ehrenreich extended a rousing challenge to women. Because of gender inequity, they stated,

today even our familiar list of feminists' economic reforms—day care, affirmative action, and the more radical demand for equal pay for comparable work—begins to look inadequate to the circumstances.

We need a feminist economic program, and that is no small order. An economic program that speaks to the needs of women will have to address some of the most deep-seated injustices of a business-dominated economy and a male-dominated society. Framing it will take us beyond the familiar consensus defined by the demand for equal rights—to new issues, new problems, and maybe new perspectives. Whether there are debates ahead or collective breakthroughs, they are long overdue: the feminization of poverty demands a *feminist* vision of a just and democratic economy.

Questions for Reflection

1. Looking at your list of possible basic causes, was there anything in your vision of new economic arrangements which might alter these root level problems?

2. Stallard and Ehrenreich conclude that "the feminization of poverty demands a *feminist* vision of a just and democratic economy." Based on your experience in everyday life and in envisioning a new economic arrangement, do you see any reason to believe that a feminist vision of an economic system is more likely to be just and democratic than our present one? Explain your answer with specific examples from your experience and/or dreams and visions.

Entering Into Sources of Hope Offered by Other Women

In an article "Women and the State: Ideology, Power, and the Welfare State," Frances Fox Piven says:

There is reason to think a mass movement of women is emerging in the United States. The movement is broad and multifaceted; it includes women from all classes, and takes diverse political forms reflecting the very different social locations of its constituents. Nevertheless it is unified in raising a credible challenge to current policy on the military, the economy, social welfare, and the environment. I believe the emergence of women as active political subjects on a mass scale is due to the new consciousness and new capacities yielded women by their expanding relationships to state institutions.

Piven moves on to analyze some of the factors responsible for the emerging gender gap, reflected in public opinion polls and in voting behavior, which indicates a sharpening divergence of attitude and belief between women and men.

The emphasis on peace, economic equality, and social needs associated with the gender gap suggests the imprint of what are usually taken as traditional female values. This frequently made

observation suggests that the gender gap is not a fleeting response to particular current events, but that it has deep and authentic roots in the longstanding beliefs of women. . . .

The scale of the gender gap, and the fact that it has persisted and widened in the face of the Reagan administration's ideological campaign, suggests the enormous electoral potential of women. This, of course, [was] the media's preoccupation, and the preoccupation of contenders in the 1984 election as well. But its importance extends beyond 1984. Women have moved into the forefront of electoral calculations because they are an enormous constituency that is showing an unprecedented coherence and conviction about the key issues of our time, a coherence and conviction which I have argued owes much to the existence of the welfare state. This electorate could change American politics. . . . The growing politicization of American women suggests that the electoral and organizational support needed to nourish and sustain movements, and to yield them victories, is potentially enormous.

NETWORK is a social-justice lobby started by women. A highly respected effort within the Christian community, it represents recent action by women concerned about a more just and caring society, which provides organizational support needed by many caring and concerned persons.

NETWORK: Life, Faith, and Action as One Piece

NETWORK is a Catholic social-justice lobby in Washington, D.C., which was started in 1971 by a group of Catholic sisters. It struggles to bring about change by influencing national legislation. The central idea behind NETWORK is a cooperative effort between grass roots and the national staff. Grassroots groups are organized to gather information and interact with Congresspersons and their constituents at the congressional district and state levels. At the national level, the staff coordinates these groups, provides needed information, and communicates with Congresspersons and their staffs—at times in coalition with other public-interest organizations such as IMPACT, a similar kind of organization for some Protestant denominations.

Besides its legislative efforts, NETWORK has also been working to create a life-style that reflects its concern for a socially just society. The values of scripture, specifically its call to justice, not only influence the issues NETWORK members espouse but also shape their way of life. In an effort to articulate this religious dimension, the staff began a series of reflection days. For nine years now they have been involved in a process of discovering how their faith and values relate to their life, including work styles and the organization as a whole. Among the values they have explored and developed from their experience are participation, integration, mutuality, and stewardship. These values, the staff believes, are important not only for the life and activity of NETWORK but also for the more just society they work toward. Consequently, a central goal of their reflective process is to give shape to this preferred future world, while trying to actualize it in NETWORK by making the organization an alternative to things as they are.

For NETWORK, participation means that persons are actively involved in all that affects their lives. It implies that those making decisions experience the consequences of those decisions and are accountable for them. When NETWORK evaluated its structure against participation as a value, they had to acknowledge that they were not practicing what they preached; their organizational model was hierarchical. Consequently, a process to change their structural model from vertical lines to circles was initiated. They started to share responsibility and decision making more completely, to struggle through to consensus, to cooperate better, to work through conflict, to become excited about one another's challenges and victories, to come through for one another at times of particular pressure, to understand and accept each person's gifts and insufficiencies in order to complement one another. What began as a struggle eventually became more natural. Their operational style continues to evolve.

Participative management is one way NETWORK has promoted the feminist values of cooperation and mutuality. There is no organizational "top," no dichotomy between support and professional staff or alignment of jobs on prestige basis. Responsibility is shared for the less attractive and more time consuming jobs. In this effort NETWORK is striving to enflesh a future that transforms all domination/ submission relationships into ones of cooperation and mutuality. In addition, there is a flexible work environment so that people can arrange their own work time. They trust one another to keep the tension in balance between personal needs and rhythms and those of the organization. Most importantly, they revere one another: the person, gifts, and skills each brings to NETWORK.

The NETWORK office also tries to model stewardship—nurturing personal and collective resources responsibly, with a concern for what is *needed,* not what the staff would *like* to have. Unlike business, which frequently describes efficiency as

bigger and better, the staff works at alternative ways of being efficient through careful organization, maximum cooperation, and effective planning. For example, equipment is shared not only among the staff but also with other groups whenever possible.

NETWORK members use religious symbols and ritual in their reflective process and organizational life because they are convinced of their power to integrate all of life and to affect the structural changes our society so urgently needs today. They see the power of ritual as coming chiefly from its ability to combine meaning and emotion. That combination involves people, influences them, and changes them as it puts them in touch with a deeper reality. NETWORK members are not merely trying to create a more just world out there; they are also trying to mirror it in their present personal and corporate life. Thus life becomes a whole piece as faith, life, activity, and structure are integrated.

Getting in Touch with Additional Information Available to You

1. Make a survey of recent newspaper and magazines. Cut out any articles you find that would support or question Piven's conclusion that there is "an unprecedented coherence and conviction about the key issues of our time" among women. Talk with your friends and acquaintances to discover whether they are aware of such a coherence.

2. What kind of organizational support is presently available or might be engendered to help women concerned about economic justice to actualize the electoral power they have—which Piven thinks "is potentially enormous"?

3. Think about organizations you are a part of or know something about. Try to identify each organization's basic beliefs or motives. Now look at how the organization operates. Does this operation reflect the basic beliefs of the organization? What about your church? Explain why you think such a coherence is or is not important.

4. Think about your own life. At this time, how fully does your style for living and your actions reflect your core values and beliefs?

5. Make a survey of your area. What initiatives or transforming actions are under way that seek to make our society more caring and just?

SECTION 10

Women on the Move

In this section, we will be searching for ways women's visions of more just, humane, and equitable economic arrangements can be used to nourish positive changes in our present economic order. First we will look at some concrete actions some women have already taken to transform their participation in the economic sphere. Then you will make a decision about your own compassionate work for justice, equity, and greater fullness of life.

Reflections on the Power to Live

In Section 7, we looked at the generative power of visions. The King James Version translates Proverbs 29:18 as "Where there is no vision, the people perish." Consider this statement and then write your own understanding of why visions are necessary for individuals as well as for communities, nations, and indeed the global community.

The Revised Standard Version translates the same verse as "Where there is no prophecy the people cast off restraint." In the Jerusalem Bible the verse reads, "Where there is no vision the people get out of hand."

What relationships do you find between prophetic gifts and vision? Between people getting out of hand and perishing? What insights do the last two translations add to your first statement about visions?

Entering Into the Stories of Others Who Are Acting on Vision

Some women not only have envisioned change in our present way of structuring and living our economic life but have initiated action based on their visions. Following are four examples of innovative action taken by women. One of them, the Ruether article, is an example of analysis and vision that can give rise to change.

After you have read the articles, reflect on the following questions in relation to each.

1. What implications does this model have for changes that are needed for a transformation of society?

2. How would it help avoid the feminization of poverty?

3. How would it help alleviate hunger and poverty within our nation? Within the world?

Alternatives to Crisis Living

The Survivors' Network, an organization of energetic, positive-minded Atlanta women, is dedicated to combating many of the challenges brought about by inflation and the threatened dissolution of the family unit with a support system.

The motto of the Network, "Neglect not the gifts of God within you," expresses the foundation of this organization. "Putting the Holy Spirit before us and raising the consciousness of each one of us," says Barbara A. Greene, one of the founders of the Network and a ministerial student, "is where our strength comes from."

After taking note of the devastating effects of inflation and Reaganomics on a number of people in their community, especially single-parent households, Barbara and Nancy Lyman decided to band together with other members of the community to design a plan for minimizing these effects on themselves and their families. Barbara, a staff assistant at the Presbyterian Center, says, "The Network recaptures the lost spirit that prompted our ancestors to pull together with other members of the community to assure that the basics of food, clothing, and shelter were adequately furnished for all. This sharing of essentials fostered greater love and harmony in the community, so much of which is sadly escaping our busy, sophisticated society today."

To assist them in their economic survival, the Network has presented experts in the fields of investments, accounting, insurance, real estate, and travel at their bi-weekly meetings. They also exchange newspaper and magazine clippings featuring tips on how to survive in these changing times, as well as recipes for low-cost, nutritious meals. A prosperity-consciousness workshop has blossomed as an offshoot of the parent organization, as has a cleaning and yard service.

While mastering the art of staying economically afloat, the sisters also emphasize spiritual awareness, cooperation, self-esteem, and physical well-being as a part of their program. Examples of projects presently under way to help them develop even more beauty from the inside out are body ecology/weight control, behavior modification/self-esteem/meditation, female awareness, face and hair designs, fashions, creative body language, and Bible and truth studies, especially for children. There is harmony and cohesion in their efforts, so the energy generated by this group as a whole is likely to enable them to achieve their goals.

Another important factor of the Network is its financial scope. Presently, its "kitty" could become available to a Network sister on an emergency-loan basis. There is also an educational fund which the sisters intend to use for the education of their own children, but from which contributions to such agencies as the United Negro College Fund are also made.

Although there are no men in the Survivors' Network, there are some unofficial "brothers" to the group, and fraternal network organizations are being encouraged. "We feel we can be more helpful in the lives of men if we get ourselves together first," says Barbara. "The growth we experience as women and as individuals will also benefit men, whether they are our husbands, boyfriends, fathers, or sons. We also feel that love is not finding the right person but *being* the right person."

The Survivors' Network is currently alive with ideas, energy, and determination for the future. Projects are on the drawing board from canning and freezing to homemade Christmas gifts. It is hoped that other sister groups can be formed in as many cities as there is need for such an organization.

One Woman's Initiative

SELFHELP Crafts is a marketing outlet for skilled craftspeople from many developing countries around the world. The name comes from one of its main goals—to help persons earn a living through traditional crafts. SELFHELP Crafts is a program of Mennonite Central Committee (MCC), a relief and service agency supported by Mennonites and Brethren in Christ throughout the United States and Canada.

SELFHELP Crafts began in the late 1940s when Edna Ruth Byler brought home a few pieces of needlework from Puerto Rico to sell and take orders, thus providing supplemental income for women with embroidery skills. Following the 1947 war in Israel and Jordan, a similar program was begun taking orders for needlework made by Palestinian refugee women.

In the 1960s, crafts from a woodworking cooperative in Haiti were added to the program. In 1970 the gift shop and center for marketing activities moved from Mrs. Byler's home to the new MCC Material Aid warehouse near Ephrata, Pennsylvania.

The Canadian division operating on a provincial basis was centralized in 1981 when modern warehouse facilities and a retail store opened in New Hamburg, Ontario. The U.S. program relocated in its own SELFHELP Crafts Center in 1982. In a twenty-year period, annual sales have increased from $1,815 to over $2 million.

Working Women and the Male Workday
Rosemary Ruether

One essential element in the feminist struggle for equality is the demand for equal work roles, equal opportunities on the job, equal pay for equal work. This demand encounters great resistance from both employers and male labor leaders, in part because of cultural prejudices about the male's higher prestige. Women are treated as a surplus labor force, to be drawn upon when the need for labor is expanding or in wartime. They are structured into different supportive roles, such as typing, for male executives—roles that fall at a markedly lower level of prestige and pay. They are hired and fired with much less job protection. And throughout it all the myth is preserved that "all" women belong at home as wives and mothers and work only for "extras." Above all, women should not compete with men for the same jobs and pay.

All this is well documented by feminist analysis. What seems to me not yet adequately treated is the component of this pattern that is systemic to the very organization of work and that cannot be solved by attacking cultural stereotypes alone. Or rather, the cultural stereotypes are the ideological superstructure of a certain economic system and cannot be changed without reorganizing that system.

One problem with women's demand for equal pay for equal work is that it generally continues to presuppose the male workday, which was shaped during the period of industrialization when work became dissociated from family-run shops and farms. Men and women in the preindustrial family could share work to a greater extent because the means of production were owned by and located near to the home. Industrialization took the means of production out from primary communities into collectivized systems owned by the capitalist. Women progressively lost their role in productive labor, and male and female roles were defined in mutually exclusive patterns that separated work and home to a much greater extent than had previously been the case.

Despite the numbers of poorer women who also worked in factories, productive work—which took people to a distant place for the daylight hours of each workday—began to be defined as belonging exclusively to men. Women were segregated into child-raising, consumer management, and housework. Male and female functions were seen as the opposite halves of a complementary system that allowed neither sex to participate very much in the sphere of the other.

The man's workday was organized on the presupposition that he had a wife who performed all auxiliary functions for him, thereby freeing him for exclusive attention to the "job." It was also assumed that one salary was sufficient for the corporate unit of husband, wife, and children. Successful male prowess on the job meant a sufficient income to send the wife home to be full-time housewife. The man whose wife "had to go out to work" because of financial need was humiliated.

Great contradictions arise when women try to integrate themselves into a work world organized on these assumptions. Having no wives, women must try to do two jobs at once, to be in two places at once, to the detriment of both. If they aspire to a real "career" in competitive professional employment, they conclude that they better not marry or at least better not have children.

Women who don't want to make these sacrifices try to change the home pattern by insisting on sharing domestic work with their husbands. But this effort encounters constant resistance from a work pattern that says a man should not have to work "all day" and then come home to make his own bed, shop for or cook his own meals, wash his own dishes, or change a baby's diaper. I believe that this pattern cannot be changed very much simply by power and cultural struggles on the domestic front. For the presupposition of this resistance to shared housework is still the male workday.

The Relation of Salary to Family

Feminism must reckon explicitly with the corporate purpose of the salary, which relates salary to the support not just of an isolated individual but of family units of dependent persons who are not salaried. Women's demand for equal pay for equal work generally ignores this purpose and treats the salary individualistically; each person is said to be entitled to the same pay level for the same work regardless of the living unit that is to be supported or the salary's relation to other incomes.

It is understandable that feminists don't want to raise the potential conflict between individualistic and corporate ways of looking at work income. For the corporate relation of income to family is usually used against women; it is said that women's work is a "second income"; that, therefore, women don't need the same pay; that they should take second place in employment, etc.

Feminists answer that many working women are unmarried or are single-parent heads of households. However, the fact that many working women are in this situation doesn't change the reality that most working women do belong to two-income households. It is precisely this latter kind of family that must be analyzed in terms of its overall socioeconomic effects.

The relation of salary to family is crucial to the resistance to equal pay for women. An unwillingness to see that some families have dual incomes while others suffer male unemployment is a key element to the constant defeat of women in the capitalist job market. When women seek equal pay and job opportunities without seeking also to change the workday and the social function of income, several things tend to happen. A token number of elite women become display cases of equal employment in various professions. They are able to compete on the job by having few or no children and/or the money to pay others for household work and child care. . . .

Since now the economy is not increasing its job opportunities fast enough to supply jobs for all who want them, the struggle for equal job opportunities is going on at the same time that men, both workers and professionals, are experiencing rising unemployment. Expanding opportunities for women are, therefore, obtained in direct competition with men.

In some cases this may mean that white middle-class women are pushing black and brown men out of work. Just as the older women's movement of the early twentieth century tended to ignore its class context and so allowed itself to be used to increase the political power of the WASP ruling class through the franchise (while disenfranchising blacks), so there is some danger that the women's movement of today may become a means of extending the income of the white middle-class family through the double income while lower-class brown and black families suffer 30 percent unemployment.

Employment for women purchased at the expense of unemployment for men in the *same* class level also tends to bring about a reaction. It is again asserted that one income is sufficient for one family and that men have the prior right to the job. Thus women's gains in employment remain token: flashy appearances of exemplary individuals in various professions. But for most women the use of females as surplus and marginal labor, last hired and first fired, continues.

Attacking the Wrong End of the Stick

One key to unlocking this dilemma is to recognize explicitly the systemic relations of home and work and to devise a means of adjusting *both sides* of this equation. We need to change a pattern of complementary and mutually exclusive roles of work and home to one of shared work for both men and women on both sides of the home—work split.

The tendency of both feminism and socialism in response to the dilemma of work is to attack "the nuclear family" as the root of the problem. . . .

All these solutions [such as paying women for homemaking and institutionalizing child care and food preparation] attack the wrong end of the stick; namely, the home rather than the industrial work pattern. I would like to imagine a different system where men and women are presumed to share equally both the world of jobs, of public power and experience, and the work of the private sphere, which means not just housework, child-raising, and consumer management but all the opportunities for self-cultivation that the leisure sphere offers. This is also where time is our own, where it is not incorporated into a wage system we don't control that owns and manages our lives.

The 25-Hour Work Week

One essential element in changing the present work–home dichotomy is to change the male workday that makes these two spheres mutually exclusive. Therefore, let us play, somewhat arbitrarily, with an alternative pattern. Suppose that for those families or living units of two adult wage earners a normal work week was 25 hours rather than 40. This would allow the two working adults to adjust differently their roles in relation to each other. The 25-hour week could be divided into a 6¼-hour four-day work week or an 8¼-hour three-day work week. Collectively the couple (which might or might not be a heterosexual married couple) would work 50 hours, bringing home a proportionately higher income than the one 40-hour income but not so much as to create the present violent maladjustments between some families with two incomes and others with none.

With a three- or four-day flexible work week, there is much more possibility of mutually shared housework and child-raising. Each person could be home one or two days while the other is working. Each would feel less pressed to find time for civic activity, self-cultivation, relation to children, etc. The pattern of overworked husbands and understimulated wives could be changed in a real and systemic way to one of mutually shared work and home lives.

Presently what are called "part-time" jobs are only available in some professions, such as teaching, and usually put the worker in a much inferior position in terms of pay scale, benefits, job advancement, etc. Essential to the flexible work week is that it would be paid on the same proportional pay scale as a longer work week and would put the worker in the same track for retirement and medical benefits, advancement, etc. For example, instead of one adult holding a 40-hour job paying $20,000, both would hold 25-hour jobs paying $12,500 each, collectively earning $25,000 per year for a 50-hour week.

Someone who needs a longer work week would not be forced to work a shorter one. Particularly, single persons or single-parent households might opt for the longer work week. This approach still offers some benefits to the multiple-income family, but not quite the overwhelming disparity we now have between the two-income childless family and the one working parent with dependent children. Tax breaks and child-care subsidies would also be available to the one-parent household with dependent children.

But above all, income would not be dealt with individualistically, in a way that ignores the relation of income to family support. The present possibility of a double income for a few elite professional couples may seem a great advantage to a few women. But it can only mean defeat for the majority of women and injustice for the larger work force. If we hope to change systemically the present subjugation of women in the home, the entire system of work must be adjusted for shared roles and incomes on both sides of the home–work relation.

A shared 50-hour work week would not abolish the need for child care for preschool children. We assume that if they are also to have time together, husband and wife would be working some days at the same time. We also must question the assumption that the isolated nuclear family, where one lone adult is related exclusively to one or more preschool children, is the ideal way to socialize small children. If women do not like their isolation with small children, it should be evident that children don't particularly like it either. Two-year-olds like to be with other two-year-olds, with an adult or two as a nearby resource but not as a constant companion.

The isolation of small children from a peer group or from adults other than the mother also is a peculiar result of industrialization. It was not a pattern made in the Garden of Eden: it is not normative historically, nor should it be presumed to be particularly good for children. Indeed, a lot of the frustration that builds up between a mother and one or two small children alone together is that children also are unhappy with a situation that isolates them from other children and adults in the tribal community that has been the normal environment for child socialization for most of human history.

We need group child care, and not just as a way of freeing mothers from other work or from their entrapment in the home, although these are perfectly appropriate results. Child care also should not be seen as parents' desire to repudiate their responsibilities as the primary child-raisers nor should the child-care unit be seen as "handing over the child to an impersonal institution." Rather, we should understand this need as a way of recollectivizing child-raising and recovering some of the attributes of the tribal community.

Resocialization of child care could be done either on the job or in the neighborhood. On-the-job care has many advantages. Work ceases to be seen as exclusive of the sphere of home and children. Facilities set up within the shop, university, or factory mean that children can go with one or both parents to work, can be visited on and off during the workday, can themselves have a sense of knowing about and participating in the parents' work world, and can come home with their mother or father at night. The preindustrial child could hang around the father's blacksmith shop and could feel that he or she knew what "Daddy" did at work, whereas the modern child is as cut off as women from access to the "man's" world. On-the-job child care could be paid for partly from parent's wages and partly by the employer.

Toward Some Markedly Different Values

A second pattern of child care could occur in the neighborhood. Here a group of parents could collaborate. Perhaps fifteen parents from eight families (including one single-parent family) with a total of sixteen preschool children between them could pool the work. Three parents each day, on a rotating basis, would run the facility, each contributing one day a week. Communities might also develop training centers with paid professionals to give such parents help in developing skills.

Such neighborhood groups would mean that larger groups of children would grow up together as something like extended families. They could not only see each other during day care but also form bonds on a continuing basis, much as traditional African villages bond groups of children together from an early age into a primary peer group. These children would also have the enrichment of having not just two parents but an extended group of "aunts" and "uncles" to whom they could look for additional adult resources and role models. This is particularly valuable for children as they enter teenage years.

Not only would such family bonding be enormously helpful support for parents, but it would be a much more satisfying community for children that would diffuse much of the sibling rivalry and child–parent antagonism typical of the isolated nuclear family. This has to do not with abolishing the family and relation to one's own parents, brothers, and sisters as a primary base of identity and affection, but simply with embedding the family in a larger supportive network.

These are very modest suggestions. A 50-hour work week shared by two adults and collective child care in neighborhoods and workplaces are possibilities that one could start to work on in many places *now*. Yet the development of such patterns add up to an enormous shift in the present pattern of mutually exclusive male–female, work–home dichotomies that makes such simple matters as shared housework, inexpensive, noninstitutional child care, and job opportunities for women insoluble within the present system.

Such developments would work no enormous dislocation in the social patterns that Americans are comfortable with, but they would extend and build on the best aspects of our present arrangements. This means, I think, that there are truly possible solutions *for us* unlike Israeli kibbutzim and Chinese peasant communes that might sound great but have little chance of widespread success for people with our history and society.

There are embedded in these changes some values and assumptions that are markedly different from those of the present American capitalist society. First of all, we assume that all people in a society have a right to work and to a living wage. We assume that the total productive resources of a society belong first of all to the whole society, rather than to the owners who use them privatistically to maximize profits at the expense of the common good. A *planned* society is necesary to organize work and wage patterns so that all adults receive both regular jobs and a living wage.

I believe this also means that the extreme discrepancies between business executives who receive $225,000 a year and the one family in eight whose income falls below the poverty level, such as presently obtains in our society, must be brought to an end. Wages should be redistributed, not just through taxes (which is annoying to people and wastes a lot of money in bureaucracy), but through changing the extreme gaps in wages. At present costs of living, a full-time working family should perhaps earn no less than $18,000 and no more than $50,000. Some hierarchy of wages, sense of "advancement," and success would still be preserved through wages, but not with the present extremes. Many people would find their sense of advancement and success through means other than wages, hopefully through means that encourage mutual help rather than win-lose antagonisms in society.

A New Kind of Office Politics
Dan Marschall

In one of the ironic satisfactions that American culture occasionally produces, Hollywood writers arrived in Cleveland, Ohio, last fall to interview scores of women office workers who have been discriminated against, underpaid, sexually harassed, unfairly fired, or otherwise mistreated on the job. Their stories provided the grist for a new television series . . . *9 to 5*, a spin-off of the 1980 movie in which three rebellious office workers strike back at their piggish boss. The series . . . like the film, uses a mixture of humor and sarcasm to depict the office environment.

How has the everyday reality of office work come to attract so much attention? Major credit must go to organizers like Karen Nussbaum, the dynamic leader of a nationwide organization of clerical workers called Working Women. . . .

Nussbaum made labor history last spring when

she announced that her group was entering into a unique partnership with the Service Employees International Union (SEIU), a 675,000-member union of hospital and public employees, to conduct joint organizing campaigns. The vehicle for these efforts is District 925, a nationwide union local also led by Nussbaum (as president) and staffed by organizers drawn directly from the working women's movement.

After ten years of organizing, Nussbaum believes that she is now on the verge of a new breakthrough. The labor movement's great organizing drives of the 1930s concentrated on men in basic industries like steel and auto; at the time, women were a much smaller percentage of the labor force. In the following decades, as women surged into the labor pool, most unions were either too shortsighted or too sexist to organize the new workers—or even to recognize them *as* workers. Clerical jobs were regarded as pleasant, ladylike occupations and women as transitional, almost unnecessary members of the work force.

Even as late as 1975, when Nussbaum first met with local union officials in Boston, the response to organizing "ranged from incredulity to those who laughed right in our faces," she recalls. "One union representative said, 'The reason that you can't organize office workers is because women think with their crotch, not their brain.' It was not a really warm reception!"

But now, the union movement itself is in deep trouble. Unionized workers comprise only about 20 percent of the labor force—the lowest level since 1942—and the clout of the labor movement is declining. At a time when no growth is expected in the most heavily unionized economic sectors, labor is bargaining away previously won benefits in order to keep its members employed at all. In the meantime, office work has mushroomed and now constitutes 57 percent of nonagricultural occupations, and white-collar work is expected to grow by about 9.4 million jobs by 1990. What this means is clear: "The viability of the trade union movement in large part will depend on its success in organizing the growth jobs, chief among them being clerical work," Nussbaum stresses. And that means that labor will have to come to terms with the impact of feminism during the 1970s: "We're organizing not just as workers but as women. We'll address the problems that women face. We'll bring with us our own women leaders and our success on issues of concern to women."

Nussbaum herself was an office worker who first found employment compiling loose-leaf notebooks for the Harvard University School of Education. "One day I was sitting in my office and it was noontime," she remembers. "One of the students walked in, looked all around, and then looked me dead in the eye and said: 'Isn't anybody here?' This was really fuel for the fire."

That kind of disrespect, on top of low pay and nonexistent benefits, led to the formation of the Harvard Office Workers' Group and, later, to a citywide version dubbed "9 to 5." Nussbaum realized that clerical workers needed their own unique form of organization—one that drew on the consciousness of the women's movement and used direct-action techniques of community organizing, along with lawsuits and appeals, to pressure discriminatory employers.

9 to 5 was the prototype, and as the model spread to other cities, Karen Nussbaum became a leading figure in the working women's movement. . . . She is the executive director of Working Women, which has its headquarters in Cleveland, where she lives with her husband, Ira Arlook, a director of a national citizens' group called Citizen Action. Nussbaum leads an organization with more than 12,000 members, 23 local affiliates, and a full-time staff of 50. Staff members are paid no higher than the prevailing wages for women workers. . . .

Still in its childhood, District 925 has yet to win any big elections, although campaigns encompassing some 15,000 clericals are proceeding in universities, insurance firms, legal offices and major corporations. Already more than a thousand persons have called the district's hotline (800-424-2936) to ask about unionizing. At the Equitable Life Assurance Society in Syracuse, New York, for example, a worker heard a two-minute radio blurb by Nussbaum and spent six weeks searching for District 925. When an organizer came out, she met with a small group of employees and formed a 15-person, secret, internal committee that held a dozen educational sessions covering the company, union-busting methods, the make-up of the union, and organizing strategy. This group process, a hallmark of the district's feminist-oriented approach, knitted the internal committee into a strong unit, helping to give the workers the confidence that they could indeed challenge their employer on his own turf.

They needed that extra self-confidence. As soon as the committee began circulating union authorization cards, the company turned to an increasingly popular tactic: it hired a high-powered consulting firm that specializes in modern psychological management techniques to perform the old-fashioned task of union-busting. In this case, the tactic failed and the organizers won their election. Still, many employers are determined to keep the unions out, and most have been quite effective: less than 50 percent of white-collar organizing drives succeed. In that context, District 925's $1 million annual budget for national organizing seems paltry.

Nussbaum knows the difficulties, but she remains firmly optimistic. "Our job in the '70s was to have a public debate about the rights of office workers. And we've won the debate. There is widespread agreement that discrimination characterizes the modern office. Now we're in a position in the '80s to begin the job of organizing."

It might be that the woman whose movement coined the slogan "Raises, Not Roses!" was predestined for her role: Karen Nussbaum was born on National Secretaries Day.

After this article was written, Equitable announced its plans to close down the Syracuse office. Nussbaum's office commented:

An ad hoc Syracuse-based coalition formed a "Keep Our Jobs Here" campaign to publicize and protest the detrimental effects of the threatened office closing on the Syracuse community.

Scores of unions ceased long-standing business with Equitable or refused to enter into new business with the company, and the *boycott brought results:*

In September of 1983—after 20 months of NLRB violations—Equitable notified District 925 and the media that it intended to recognize and bargain with the union.

But the agreement to bargain is only the first step. The company has failed to come to terms on a contract for the workers and continues to unilaterally cut the workforce—20 of the original 93 to date.

And Equitable has instituted "increase productivity" standards for automated equipment that have transformed the office into a virtual factory out of the unenlightened and unorganized past.

District 925 is redoubling its efforts on the boycott until a fair contract is negotiated—a contract which includes assurances of the Syracuse workers' jobs.

The boycott which still continues, was adopted because:

Equitable discriminates against women as consumers by basing its insurance policy on gender.

Equitable discriminates against its employees through a policy of anti-unionism and through personnel policies that allow sex and age discrimination.

The insurance industry has made a handsome profit at the expense of low-wage women who do the bulk of insurance work—typing, filing, claims processing. The industry opposes employees' efforts to improve their working conditions and job status, including unionization, which requires employers to collectively bargain with employees and loosens the reins of the employer's unilateral control.

And currently, the United States Equal Employment Opportunity Commission (EEOC) has a lawsuit pending against Equitable charging the company with age discrimination arising from the layoffs of over 550 employees in 1978 and 1979.

Getting in Touch with Your Own Action Possibilities

In view of the magnitude of various aspects of the economic crisis confronting the nation and world, it would be easy just to give up and take the stance indicated by Estragon in Beckett's *Waiting for Godot.*

Vladimir: Well? What do we do?
Estragon: Don't let's do anything; it's safer.

The only way to counteract this kind of powerlessness paralysis, which you may feel especially if you are doing this study alone, is to risk stepping out on faith—to initiate some beginning action to bring some needed change, even if you don't have all the facts, even if the way seems unsure. Your action may seem fairly small and insignificant, or it may be of major consequence. It may be an individual or a corporate action. It may be to try to influence legislation for major structural changes, or it may be to help empower, stand with, or provide relief for some victims of our present economic arrangements. Action could take the form of involving others in consciousness-raising studies similar to this one. It might be to identify and join with other organized women's coalitions and lobbying groups that are already working for structural change. It might be to organize such a group. It might be to decide on some new action(s) that would bring individual or corporate life-style change. It might be to dream a new dream and to begin enfleshing it in everyday life, thereby offering a new alternative to the way work and economic life is presently carried out.

Regardless of its form, it is important that some action directed toward the attainment of economic justice for women, in this country or internationally, be initiated. Without such a beginning, your concern is stillborn. From one undertaking, others can follow, even if the initial action appears to be one small step into a massive and confusing wilderness.

Questions for Reflection

1. After taking a few moments to center yourself, using one of the relaxation exercises suggested in Section 1, envision what you would most like to do. Don't set any limitations on your thoughts, such as "I could never do that!" or "That's too idealistic!" Just dream big, without exercising any evaluative judgment. That can come later.

What one individual action in your personal life and one communal action would you most like to take to move toward greater economic justice for yourself and others of our global family? Write them down.

2. Now turn to "What Can You Do About It?" (page 41). Does this material suggest additional actions you want to take?

3. Take time to think and look in your telephone and church directories. Are there existing women's coalitions or lobbies that are already at work on some of the concerns you have chosen: a local League of Women Voters, a worker or consumer cooperative, a group offering alternative child care, a "Bread for the World" group, an economic or hunger task force, an alliance for welfare mothers, a peace or nuclear freeze group? You might also need to make a few phone calls to your church and to local governmental agencies, such as the Department of Welfare, Human Services, etc. Check through the Justice for Women Working Groups listed in the Resource section for additional sources of information. It may be that your first step will be to join others already at work on economic justice.

4. After you have gathered information about existing organizations, it is time to use your evaluative judgment to make your action decisions. Consider who you are—your desires and dreams, your gifts, abilities, potentials, and needs—your community and opportunities it offers, connections you have in the church and community, and so on.

Refine your list of possibilities, searching for a few beginning steps. Then consider each in light of the following:

To what degree does this action move toward greater economic justice for myself and/or other women and consequently all human beings?

How much time and power do I have to carry out or facilitate this action?

If your action is not an individual action and if it does not involve joining in an ongoing group work, consider whom you might enlist to help you.

5. In light of the above, make your final decision about what you will do. Write your commitment to action here and get started.

A Closing Prayer

God, make me an instrument of your peace;
Where there is hatred, let me sow love;
Where there is injury, pardon;
Where there is doubt, faith;
Where there is despair, hope;
Where there is darkness, light;
Where there is sadness, joy.

O Divine God, grant that I may not so much seek
To be consoled, as to console;
To be understood, as to understand;
To be loved, as to love.
For it is in giving that we receive;
It is in pardoning that we are pardoned;
And it is in dying that we are born to eternal life.

AMEN

(Prayer of St. Francis of Assisi)

LEADER'S GUIDE

Women, Faith,
and Economic Justice

CONTENTS

Introduction

The introduction to the workbook warns readers that they will not be given all the information needed for their study. This is a process guide: The underlying principle here is *to motivate and enable women to uncover, discover, and create for themselves as much of the content as possible.* Women will be involved in a *process* of growing in awareness of their own involvement in and knowledge of economic practices and systems and they will also begin to trace and analyze the effects of that economic involvement for their own lives and the lives of others in the global community; they will be doing Bible study, which assumes that they can do their own theological reflection about the relationship of faith and economics; and they will be encouraged to envision alternative ways of arranging economic life and decide upon basic changes which are needed if we are to create more humane and just economic relationships.

This process of discovery was decided upon for several reasons.

1. Economics is a complex and complicated subject. It is easy to overwhelm study members by providing too many data too soon. As individuals become involved in the process of pinpointing what they already know about economic realities, they are energized to learn more and will be motivated to gather their own information as they need it and are ready for it.

2. Many facts about current economic realities and events are quickly outdated, so a great deal of information has not been included. Rather, the Resources section indicates places to go for information that can supplement daily newspapers and regular women's and news magazines.

3. Economics is a potentially explosive issue because for many people in the United States the capitalistic system is our holy cow. Consequently, we may not be open to hearing about how women have been exploited by that system or how much affluence in this country is directly related to economic exploitation of Third World peoples, nations, and resources. We are more likely to be able to see and analyze the causes of economic oppression if we discover that reality ourselves through our own stories and the stories of others.

In a climate of openness, acceptance, and freedom, as women learn from other women and think through for themselves the way economic realities have affected their perceptions, attitudes, relationships, values, goals, and even religious beliefs, they become involved in an energy-giving process that will motivate them to learn more and to act upon their learnings.

4. Since economic realities do affect the whole person, the educational process must involve the whole person—feelings as well as mind—using both to discover reasons behind feelings and actions appropriate for feelings. Indeed, it is our feelings that generate energy. With this kind of internalized learning and motivation, women are able to move beyond the negative feelings that are likely to be aroused around a consideration of economics, such as fear, anger, guilt, hostility, and powerlessness. As these feelings surface in a discovery process, they can be used to trigger new hopes, visions, and efforts toward the creation of a more just, livable, and joyful world for all, and they can unleash energy to work toward those visions.

Adapting the Study to Your Group's Needs

According to when you are carrying out this study, the time you have available, the particular group you are working with, and the goals and objectives of that group, you will need to select, expand, contract, omit, or redesign the study process to meet your individual needs.

The process is divided into four basic units: history, biblical roots, envisioning hopes, and action. Within those four parts are ten sections, which form the basis for ten two- to three-hour sessions. Two ideal settings for this study are either (1) a special study group that meets for two to three hours weekly for a period of ten to twelve weeks or (2) a two- to three-day leadership training event, retreat, or workshop, in which morning, afternoon, and night segments of time are used for the individual sessions. In a two- to three-day event, informal community building taking place during off hours would provide added impetus for a deeper kind of sharing, learning, analysis, and commitment.

If you are going to lead this study within an ongoing structure such as a women's association, task force, circle, or church school class, you will need to adapt the design carefully according to the time you have available. For example, if you have only one hour available at a time and you want to complete the entire process, you might need as many as 20 or 25 individual sessions. Or you could decide which exercises could be done individually at home and assign those portions at each session. Or you might decide to have fewer sessions; if so, you will need to pick and choose or adapt different parts of the study process. You might want to try only one or two parts of the study or only one or two sections from each of the parts.

To tailor the study to the special needs and objectives of your group requires a great deal of advance planning. There is no way to begin without proper preparation. You may want to work with a committee of three or four other women to do your basic planning and to share in group leadership functions. At any rate, you will want to consider the following:

1. Learn the needs and gifts of the different women in your group.

2. Look at the purpose of each section and create your own purpose in relation to the issue, your group, time constraints, and so on. Note especially those places where group members could be asked to report on workbook content and where outside speakers could be used.

3. Select or adapt activities from this guide or create others that are most effective in meeting your objectives for each session. Be sure to note the audiovisual possibilities listed in the Resources.

Although you will want to have an overall design in mind as you begin your study, keep that design flexible and open so that you can make adjustments according to what actually happens in each session. Remember that your group is uncovering, discovering and/or creating a major part of the content they will be dealing with. You will not always be able to predict the nature or direction of that content, so be ready to move along new avenues that seem appropriate for your group. At times this may mean inviting a guest resource person to speak on specific areas where a particular kind of content is needed. Or it may mean selecting an audiovisual resource for the job. It could mean deciding to omit particular parts of the process that appear unnecessary for your group. In any event, let what actually happens in early sessions help determine how you structure upcoming sessions.

Group Membership

It is important that the study group include women from diverse racial, ethnic, socioeconomic, cultural, and national backgrounds, insofar as is possible. This kind of pluralistic setting is extremely helpful when economic issues are being dealt with, because different individuals and groups have experienced diverse consequences of our present modes of arranging economic life. In addition, different values, beliefs, attitudes, and perceptions of the world, human life, and meaning have arisen from these varied work experiences. There is no way we can fully understand the consequences of our economic system for others until they tell us. When people from differing backgrounds begin to share their economic experiences, hopes, and dreams, quite different realities and patterns of meaning begin to emerge and interconnect and we gain new perceptions and new meanings.

Because many women's groups do not reflect the rich diversity of persons present in our nation and world, it will be necessary to do advance planning if the study is to include people from different backgrounds. In addition to considering joining with a group of women from another part of town or another church with different racial or ethnic origins, you might invite recent refugees or immigrants or international visitors to North America to attend, be they government, business, or industry employees, students, faculty, or medical personnel. Don't forget to consider members of welfare rights groups, women's lobby groups, or other women's groups that are organized around some aspect of economic life.

If it is not possible to have women from diverse backgrounds as a part of your ongoing study, consider asking several resource persons from these backgrounds to join in different sessions, either sharing in the group activity or taking part in the leadership.

Groups who find it impossible to provide a pluralistic setting for their study will have to rely heavily on the accounts of women from different backgrounds provided in Part One. The women represented in these stories—such as Gaynell Begley and Min Chong Suk—cannot talk back and answer questions, but they do provide some insight into the lives of persons who are different from the dominant culture's stereotype. You might also encourage participants to read additional stories from Studs Terkel's books *Working* and *American Dreams: Lost and Found* (see book list in Resources section).

Group Size and Arrangement

As will be obvious from the activity suggestions, a large part of this study is envisioned for small-group work, five or six persons. This is not only because of the intimate kind of sharing and learning called forth by the small group but also because of the need for active involvement if group members are really to learn; that is, do more than have someone tell them facts they will soon forget. Depending on your membership, it could be beneficial to have persons in the same group of five or six throughout the study.

This, of course, does not mean that this guide cannot be used with a group of any size. It simply means that for a major portion of your time a large group will be divided into smaller groups where sharing and learning from one another will take place. Some informational content can be given in the larger group, according to your group's need, and small groups should share their findings with the larger group.

The Learning Environment

An underlying goal of this study process is a transformation of consciousness that frees women to gain new understandings about the role economics plays in human life and the interrelationship of faith and economics. Such a transformation can occur as women begin to (1) share their economic stories, (2) ask key questions (about how economic systems influence their own and others' destinies, how economics interrelates with other public issues, and how individuals, families, and communities are controlled by economic values and systems), (3) identify which values should be the foundation of economic life, and (4) envision more just and humane economic arrangements that can make an impact on our present world. As Jackie Smith points out in *Partners in Pluralism* (pp. 10-11):

> For this to happen, fostering a warm, accepting, and free environment will be a major concern as you plan and engage in study. If women are to delve into deeper levels of self- and other-understanding, they must know that they are valued and that their attitudes, opinions, feelings, fears, and hopes will be respected. If they are to risk uncovering and sharing their own identity with others, they must feel the security of an open, nonjudgmental environment. They must sense that their discoveries will be met with deep, empathetic caring. If together the group is to confront threatening, complex, and often guilt-producing issues, it must experience an atmosphere that uses differences and conflict to find new and creative alternatives. This means that your most important function as a leader is to develop and nourish a

facilitating, caring, inclusive, and collaborative climate based on (1) basic trust in each individual as a person created in the image of God, (2) caring and careful listening for the truth of each life and world view, (3) acceptance of each person in the knowledge that each is struggling and longing for the fuller personal and corporate life God has promised, (4) acceptance of differences as an opportunity for learning and growth both in personal and corporate terms, (5) a spirit of collaboration in seeking to unearth and creatively work to overcome the injustices of our day.

To foster such an environment, you and your planning committee must set the tone by being open yourself, without masks or facades, open to learning from others and open to listening to God's spirit in your midst; being willing to explore and share your "good" and "bad" feelings and behavior; trusting your own humanness to call forth greater humanness in others; showing by your attitudes and actions that the purpose of any analysis is not to see who's wrong or who's right but rather to work together to overcome common foes; and trusting your own ability to be creatively involved with others in seeking to analyze and change destructive, divisive social structures.

Part One: Economics, Past and Present

Section 1: Beginnings

Getting Started: A major goal of this opening meeting will be for women to share with and get to know one another. After reviewing the purpose and making necessary adjustments with respect to your group, begin by sharing the purpose, overall time schedule, and design of your workshop, retreat, or course. You could use some of the thoughts listed under Reflections in your introduction. Be sure to give enough information so that the group feels at ease with what to expect. This is especially important if you are in a retreat or conference setting where information about housekeeping matters is also needed.

Since a major portion of this first session will be spent in sharing economic histories, you may not need to spend a great deal of time in personal introductions if this is not an ongoing group. With either an "old" or "new" group, you could simply ask persons to share their completion of the two suggested sentences. Allow only 1 to 3 minutes for each person's sharing.

Entering Into . . . : Read or have a member of the group read Gaynell Begley's story at an early point in your session to set the stage for writing and sharing economic histories. Gaynell reflects on her past and present life, and you will be asking group members to do the same. Her intimate reflections will trigger thoughts about the role of economic realities in personal lives and in human affairs in general. Using questions similar to the Questions for Reflection that follow Gaynell's story, lead a short discussion that will move into the next part.

Getting in Touch . . . : Have the participants get comfortable, close their eyes, and use the centering process as described. Follow by slowly reading the memory trip. Pause for a second or two at the end of each sentence so that group members can draw mental images.

Pausing a few minutes after you have read the fantasy directions, ask the group to open their eyes and return to the present. Provide opportunity for them to share with one or two persons sitting close by anything from their trip into the past they would like. Then indicate that this was an initial step in preparation for writing and sharing economic histories.

Writing and Sharing Economic Histories

Have the group turn to "Writing Your Economic History." Explain that the questions are only suggestions. Then allow 20 to 30 minutes for individual reflection and writing.

In groups no larger than six, invite each person to take 5 to 7 minutes to share their economic histories. Have a timekeeper in each group. Then have the groups reflect on what they have learned, noting similarities and differences as well as (1) relationships between economics, racism, and sexism and (2) ways these realities affect individual growth and development, perceptions, attitudes, beliefs, and values. If you have more than one small group, a few minutes should be spent in sharing one or two major insights from each group.

If time permits, conclude with a discussion centered around the similarities and differences that group members may see in the story of Gaynell and those of the group. Otherwise ask the group to reflect on this before the next session.

Section 2: How Women's Lives Are Shaped by Work and Economic Realities

Getting Started: Additional thoughts and insights about the roles economics play in human life, in the growth and development of individuals and societies, and about the relation-

ship betwen racism and sexism have occurred to participants during the interval between sessions. After a few minutes for personal sharing, read aloud "The Arithmetic of Poverty," asking for a few reactions to be shared.

Entering Into . . . : Use the paragraph preceding the two stories from Third World women to introduce this section. Read or ask two members of your group to read these stories aloud. Then use some of the Questions for Reflection to summarize findings from these real life situations.

Getting in Touch . . . : If possible use an AV such as *Controlling Interest, Sharing Global Resources,* or *Guess Who's Coming to Breakfast,* which will illustrate how material resources are produced, distributed, and controlled in our global community. Such resources will show the effects of our international system on persons such as Lucia as well as Min Chong Suk. An AV is suggested here because the relationships between overdevelopment and underdevelopment, First and Third World, poverty and affluence, and racism, sexism, and economics are complicated, interrelated, and frequently hidden. An AV can make it easier to grasp some of these complexities and interconnections. The films suggested contain factual material and study guides that will enable your group to analyze unjust production and trading structures, which help keep nations, groups (such as women and racial ethnic minorities), and individuals poor and powerless.

If an AV is out of the question, you could consider a guest speaker from a local college or university or from the business community. If neither of these suggestions is possible, allow time for participants to read silently "Around the World with Multinational Corporations."

After content presentation, allow adequate time for the group to express feelings and reactions to the information given. You may expect some expressions of disbelief or even hostility. Be sure that persons with such views are not cut off but are given adequate time to convey their concerns. Close by seeing if the group can do some summarizing as they seek to reach consensus about an appropriate end to the sentence: The primary purpose of our present economic system seems to be —————.

If the article on multinationals is not used, encourage the group to study it before the next session and to seek out additional data they may need related to feelings and concerns that surfaced in this meeting.

Section 3: Women, Hierarchy, Work, and Economics

Getting Started: After revising the purpose according to where your group is now, center your sharing around learnings, thoughts, concerns, or questions that have arisen since the last session. Then state that the central focus of this session will be to look at the nature, meaning, and purpose of work activities and the place these activities have within an economic system.

Reflections on . . . : Read aloud or have read Elizabeth Gray's statement about Western culture's eyeglasses. Following the reading, use the Questions for Reflection to enable the group to focus on the relationship between hierarchy and work activities.

Entering Into . . . : After an oral reading of Ramona Bennett's story, use some of the questions following the story to identify learnings gained.

Getting in Touch . . . : Use the Economic Consciousness Razors as a tool for allowing individuals to reflect on their present participation in economic life. Provide 20 to 30 minutes for this work. Then ask the group to study the Fact Sheet on Women and Work and The Global Picture to see if there are additions they might like to add to their statements.

Depending on time limitations, you may want to send this work home with the women and use it as the basis for a full session of sharing next time. Or, if you are in a workshop or retreat setting, it can be extended into the next segment. Use a sharing procedure similar to the one suggested in the guide to Section 1 for sharing economic histories.

Part Two: Biblical Roots

Section 4: The Jesus Movement and Economics

Getting Started: Initiate discussion of how women of biblical times may have felt about themselves as they became disciples of Jesus and active in the group of persons who followed Jesus. Read Luke 8:1–3 pointing to the inclusive nature of Jesus' ministry. Then present, in a brief lecture, the information contained in Reflections on the Role of Women or have the section read silently. In either case, following that content, enter into sharing in small groups, using the three questions that follow that section. Although the questions provide a structure

for an entire session of fruitful discussion, if your time is limited cut it off after 10 or 15 minutes and move along to the Bible study.

Entering Into . . . : State that the Bible study will take the form of a role play. If your group is large, break into smaller units of five to eight persons. Have each group present its "drama" to the total group.

The setting for the role play is the decision made in Acts 2:41–47 and 4:32–34 about economic sharing. Have the passages read and ask the group to imagine that they are hearing someone read about a decision in which they took part. In the role play, each group is to pretend that they are explaining to a woman presently outside the Jesus movement how and why they arrived at this decision. The explanation might include facts about the life-style of Jesus and his disciples and about Jesus' teachings related to what provides lasting security and the place of wealth, property, and possessions in human life. They might find it useful to divide the list of scripture passages among themselves to do about 10 minutes of refresher study before planning their role play.

Conclude the session by asking the total group to identify significant learnings from this session.

Section 5: Faith and Economics

Getting Started: Open by involving the group in a brief summary statement of what they learned about what may have motivated the earliest Christian community to share and use their possessions and wealth in a way that was radically different from the dominant economic system of the day. Then move into the session, indicating that in it you will be looking at a communal process for doing theology: that of struggling with contemporary economic realities and seeking together to discern the Spirit and will of Christ in our midst. State that in this session you will be looking at the process for "Reclaiming the Bible Through Storytelling" described by Sheila Collins.

Reflections on . . . : Allow time for individual study of Collins's article. Then, in small groups, use the three questions following the article to explore more fully the process Collins describes.

Getting in Touch . . . : Following are two ways you could involve women in a communal process of decision making about what meaning the life and teachings of Jesus have for our own day in terms of the economic realities that were uncovered in Part One. In a workshop or retreat setting, the process selected could be used in small groups following discussion of Collins's article. For weekly sessions the selected process could be used as a home assignment to share during the next meeting.

Use 1 and 2 in the workbook as work for small groups. Then using only the five final questions only of 3, have each group write its communal statement about the relationship of faith and economics. Ask them to place their statements on newsprint and post them for all to see. At the conclusion of the session, provide time for the total group to look at the faith statements on the wall.

Or use the total process suggested in Getting in Touch . . . , providing time for each individual to write an individual epistle on Faith and Economics after the small group has discussed 1 and 2. Leave time for any persons who would like to share their letters in a closing large-group session.

Section 6: Assumptions, Values, Beliefs, and Economics

Getting Started: Review the stated purpose and write your own objectives in terms of where your group is and the needs you have identified. Then have the group recall some of their learnings related to where and how God's Spirit is active in today's world to expose and overcome exploitation and to liberate God's creation for Shalom. Let the group know that in this session you will be uncovering some of the basic beliefs, convictions, and assumptions that undergird and are expressed through our contemporary economic system and work life. Note that after looking at some of these beliefs and values, the group will evaluate them against biblical values and their own theological understandings. In preparation for that evaluation, in addition to the summarizing discussion just suggested, spend some time talking about the meaning of Shalom, using the Brueggemann quote in Reflections on Shalom as a point of departure.

Next, use a centering process (similar to the one described in Section 1, Getting in Touch), pointing out that you would like participants to "see" and "hear" at their deepest level of awareness, in order to experience the fullness and joy and beauty of the interwoven, interdependent web of life communicated through the biblical vision of Shalom. Slowly read the four scripture passages. If there is time you could assign one of the listed passages to each person for silent reflection. Then, as the entire group, list the basic values and beliefs embodied in the Shalom vision.

Entering Into . . . : Have participants read silently about the assumptions drawn from our Western culture. You may find some resistance to and resentment of these statements, because they reflect the driving force that has produced what many consider to be the superior quality of life presently enjoyed by many in the United States today. Indeed, some may feel that the critique is unpatriotic because they seem to deny the validity of the utopian expectations upon which our country was founded and in which there is still great pride. But to fail to recognize destructive aspects of our communal life is, as Joanna Rogers Macy says (p. 10), to "overlook an essential element in the American character—our capacity to speak out, to 'tell it like it is.' From the time of the pilgrims we are a people who refused to be silent, who rang alarms with Paul Revere, who called for defiance with Patrick Henry, who with Abe Lincoln, Emma Goldman, Martin Luther King and countless others gave voice to the future by speaking out. But in this juncture of history, many of us muffle our concerns, shift our gaze, because we are fearful of appearing unpatriotic."

One way to expose some of the implications of these assumptions and convictions in a light, humorous manner would be to have the group spend 5 or 10 minutes in brainstorming "happiness is . . . " statements for these assumptions and for the values embodied in the Shalom vision. For example: Happiness is getting and getting; happiness is clinging to the top rung of a ladder; happiness is "naming" others. Or, on the other hand: Happiness is depending on others; happiness is sharing; happiness is being a servant. In the limited time available, conclude by having the group discuss in small groups the four Questions for Reflection. Then spend 5 minutes in a large-group session asking for a sharing of any major concerns or for learnings from their small-group work.

If you have time, individual work could be done in the six areas of "Getting in Touch . . ." with results shared in small group. When this is not possible, have that work done as an assignment, to be completed before your next session.

Part Three: Generating a New Consciousness

Section 7: Peace and Economic Security

Getting Started: In addition to the purpose stated, a major concern of this section will be to enable participants to uncover and share their feelings about the ever-present nuclear threat.

This is a difficult session to lead because of the complexity and highly technical nature of the national defense debate. Because of that complexity, from the time of Hiroshima to the recent past the debate about what amount of the national budget should be spent on the military was left up to the "experts." Now, with the phenomenal growth of military budgets and the escalation of the arms race, public debate on our national militarism has increased. However, you may find resistance to looking at essential information about the increasing threat of nuclear holocaust. As Joanna Rogers Macy points out (pp. xii, 12, xiv, 37), "The present condition and future prospects of our world engender natural, normal and widespread feelings of distress." She moves on to enumerate many cultural and psychological forces that cause us to repress or deny these responses, such as fear of pain and guilt; fear of appearing morbid, too emotional, stupid, or unpatriotic; fear of causing distress and perhaps panic; fear of actually provoking disaster by negative thinking; and so on.

On the other hand, by denying or refusing to look at the unthinkable threat in our historical period, we become paralyzed. "This repression builds a sense of fragmentation, isolation, and alienation and powerlessness [as it drains us] of energy we need for action and clear thinking." Consequently, it will be important to allow whatever time is necessary for your group to express their feelings about the information you will be providing. Macy states that when groups focus "on their felt responses to the present perils two things happen: (1) Energy is released, for it is with our feelings that our energy lies. And (2) solidarity." When participants are helped to loosen pent-up feelings, which is really pain for the world, they can more clearly see that their pain is "rooted in caring, not just for ourselves and our children, but for all of humanity." Recognizing this, they can reexperience their interconnectedness as they support and empower one another. "The realization of interconnectedness (a sense of belonging to all humanity and the web of life) . . . results in personal security and economy of effort." Macy speaks to this economy of effort in the following (p. 36):

Within the context of that larger body—or living web—our own individual efforts can seem paltry. They are hard to measure as significant. Yet, because of the systemic, interactive nature of the web, each act reverberates in that web in ways we cannot possibly see. And each can be essential to the survival of that web. In that sense every one of us can be the hundredth monkey.

Many of us know the story; it is based empirically on a scientific study. Observing the learning habits of monkeys on a remote Japanese island, anthropologists scattered sweet potatoes for them to eat. One day a monkey dropped a sweet potato in the water and, retrieving it, found it tasted better when washed free of dirt and sand. She proceeded henceforth to wash her sweet potatoes and taught her sisters to do the same. The practice spread throughout the colony. When the hundredth monkey began to wash his sweet potato in the sea, the practice appeared simultaneously on another island colony of monkeys.

Through the systemic currents of knowing that interweave our world, each of us can be the catalyst or "tipping point" by which new forms of behavior can spread. There are as many different ways of being the hundredth monkey as there are different gifts we possess. For some of us it can be through study or conversation, for others theatre or public office, for others yet civil disobedience and imprisonment. But the diversities of our gifts interweave richly when we recognize the larger web within which we act. We begin in this web and, at the same time, journey towards it. We are making it conscious.

It would be especially helpful to you if you could study Macy's book before leading this session.

With shorter sessions, use two group meetings on this subject. The first could include a statement about world militarism and a period of sharing feelings and concerns. The second would open with a discussion of the roots of world tension and conflict today, followed by An Exercise in Hope.

Reflections . . . : Begin the session by asking the group to express in couples or triads the answers to the following questions:

1. How frequently do you talk with family members or friends about your feelings or thoughts about the nuclear threat? What kind of response do you usually get, or does it vary? Do you believe it is helpful for persons to talk about the perils of living in a nuclear age?

2. When you notice headlines in the paper about budget debates over the production of

more and new weapons, etc., do you read them or move on to another item? Why?

3. In general, how would you say you react to the possibility of a nuclear holocaust?

Give 10 to 15 minutes for this personal sharing and then ask for any comments individuals would like to share with the group. Move from this discussion to content presentation. It is probably best for you not to present the information in the workbook; your primary function here is that of a creative listener who seeks to give guidance and group direction as needed. You might, however, want to share the story of the hundredth monkey to set the section within a context of hope. Then you could proceed either using one of the AVs suggested in the Resources or a guest resource person for content presentation. If you choose a speaker, be sure that she or he understands that the central focus is upon the waste to humankind of using the earth's and human resources for destructive purposes, rather than meeting human needs, and envisioning new ways of using these precious resources to provide for a real and lasting security and peace. A third alternative is simply to have participants read Reflections on World Realities silently.

In using the workbook material, state that this information focuses primarily on the role of the United States in world militarism because our country is the primary arena in which we can exercise our responsibility and the avenue through which we can exert the strongest influence. One way we have avoided looking critically at our nation's involvement in international conflict is by primarily focusing on the log in *their* eyes, whoever the other is. In this way we appear to be able to justify most of our actions, since compared to "them" we are the good guys. The result is a posture of self-righteousness that justifies much violence in the name of preserving freedom and working for peace.

Following the content presentation of your choice, open the group for general questions about the content. After 10 or 15 minutes, divide into smaller groupings and state that the primary purpose of this time together is to share feelings that have been aroused by what group members have seen or heard. If you are in a workshop or retreat setting, plan for a long break following small-group work, to provide time for some physical nourishment as well as nourishment via support the women will extend to one another.

Entering Into . . . : After the break or in a second session, begin with an oral or silent reading of the statements by Sipila and Mische. Following the reading, take 5 or 10 minutes for the group to identify primary contributions they believe women can make in working toward the goals of the Decade for Women.

Next have the information in Economic Conversion presented. You might want to plan ahead to ask a member of the group to provide this information.

Getting in Touch . . . : Introduce An Exercise in Hope with some of the thoughts contained in the first part of Getting in Touch. . . . Then divide into small groups for completion of the exercise to be done as a group rather than individually. Indicate that "Do You Know What Your Tax Dollar Buys?" and "Balancing the Budget on the Backs of Women" will help provide ideas about where this new source of resources might best be spent to provide for a lasting security.

The exercise should take 40 to 50 minutes. Ask each group to place its plan on newsprint for sharing in the closing few minutes of your total group. You might want to use the World Peace Prayer for your closing prayer.

Section 8: From Dreams and Visions to Reality

Getting Started: Review purpose and adapt as needed.

Reflections on . . . : A process used a number of times in the workbook is that of using the imagination to enlarge our world view and wisdom. Begin this session by asking the group to assess that process:

What new insights have arisen through this process?
What rays of hope have shown through some of the dark situations you have been dealing with?
What new action possibilities have been seen?
What situations from the past can you recall in which one person's hopes and dreams have brought new realities into our communal lives?

According to how this conversation goes, share as much of the content of Reflections on Envisioning as is helpful.

Next, introduce the Bible study of Paul's image of the body of Christ in 1 Corinthians 12:4–13:13, providing a brief description of the nature of the Christian community in Corinth and the possibilities for new wisdom that can be gained from this image.

Before slowly reading the passage aloud, take the group through the meditation exercise suggested, followed by the two questions. Move on to the scripture reading, waiting a few minutes in silence before asking the group to open their eyes and return to the group in awareness. If you have time, have paper and colored pens and pencils available so that individuals can make a visual or written record of images, hopes, or insights that came during this period of meditation.

Suggest that the group follow the same procedure at home, using one or more of the other passages listed.

Entering Into . . . : Either prepare a brief lecture or provide time for participants to read silently the quotations from Gilligan and Ruether. Next, initiate a discussion centered around where and when the women have been aware, in their own experience, of operating out of a "vision that everyone will be responded to and included, that no one will be left alone and hurt." Is it possible to have an ethic of care that values fullness of life for all, if human relationships are structured hierarchically? Explain.

Getting in Touch . . . : Ask individuals to find a spot where they can work by themselves. After the group has resettled, lead them in a short centering process and then, pausing after each statement or question, read the fantasy as a preparatory exercise.

Following the fantasy, ask each person to identify values reflected in their trip into the future. Provide several blank sheets of newsprint in the front of the room for individuals to write their values on, one by one. Indicate that a value already listed should not be repeated but simply marked by an * so the group can quickly see which values are most frequently listed. Then have the group break into smaller groups of two or three to share any portion of their fantasy they would like.

Envisioning . . . : If you are meeting in short sessions, this activity will need to take place in a second period of time.

Assign the task described to small groups of 5 or 6 persons; instead of being a single adviser, each group will be a committee of advisers. Be sure the task is clearly understood before turning to the Work Sheet for Creating a New Society. Instruct the groups to draw on newsprint a diagram or picture that communicates the central features of their creation after they have a rough idea of the shape their new economic arrangement will take. Allow 30 to 50 minutes for this activity.

Next, each group should be given an opportunity to briefly explain their economic arrangements for a new society. Then the group can discuss the two questions listed.

Part Four: Initiating a Process of Change

Section 9: Looking Back, Looking Forward

Getting Started: Indicate that in this first segment of the session you will be moving back from their dreams and visions for a more just and caring economic system to look at frightening aspects of a trend in our present economic situation. This is done in the midst of envisioning new possibilities in preparation for the final session, when you will be involved in selecting concrete individual and group actions in response to the present situation. It is helpful to swing back for a look at some facts before making those very important decisions.

Either have participants silently read "The Feminization of Poverty" or use its content as the basis for a lecture. After your statement or individual study, lead the group in a discussion of the two Questions for Reflection that follow the article. Provide time for thinking through the questions before entering into general discussion.

Getting in Touch . . . : In preparation for this section, it would be useful to be on the lookout for newspaper or magazine articles and cartoons that relate either to the gender gap or to a commonality of conviction about key issues among women. These could be shared, as well as the statements by Piven. In Piven's article, she also states that, until recently, the full promise of the franchise was never realized, because women "followed men" into the voting booth. She asserts that this is no longer true and that many women are voting their consciences. Ask the group about their experience. Do they find themselves less dependent on male advice in making political decisions? Are they aware of a growing coalescing of conviction among women on key issues? The July 1984 *Ms.* magazine carried an article on a Harris poll indicating that the gender gap becomes enormous when the question of voting for a woman candidate for political office is raised. How do women in your group feel about women in political office? It would give added interest to ask your group to do some surveying of your own area to see how they feel about these sorts of questions and to see if the results are similar to those of the

Harris poll. (Your library should have this back issue of *Ms.*)

After spending 15 or 20 minutes in discussion of concerns similar to those just raised, move on to consider the statement about NETWORK. Indicate that beginning with this article and continuing into the next section, you will be looking at a few innovative actions that women have initiated to bring about creative change in our common life. Looking at what others have done will help generate ideas about what actions your group may decide to take.

The story is particularly appropriate at this time in the study since NETWORK is a social-justice lobby concerned to help grass-root persons gain information and organize for legislative actions. Before the session, you could ask someone to present NETWORK's story, or have it read silently. Discussion could center around numbers 3 and 4 under Getting in Touch. Add the following question: What do you think the effects would be if more organizations sought to organize their life-styles around a concern for a more socially just and caring society?

As you close this session, encourage the group to explore what initiatives or innovative actions are occurring within your community which would eliminate some of the injustices of our present situation. Are there worker or consumer cooperatives, different arrangements for child care, or political action groups centered around justice issues?

Section 10: *Women on the Move*

Getting Started: Since you will want to allow adequate time for the decision-making process, consider breaking this section into two parts, one on models and one on the decision-making process.

Reflections . . . : After you present the three different translations of Proverbs 29:18, ask the group to form pairs and share with one other person the importance of vision in their personal lives. How does lack of vision affect their feeling about themselves, others, the world in general? Contrast this with how they feel when they are moving toward a clear vision.

Entering Into . . . : Have three persons plan beforehand to present a description of one of the models, or have the four articles read silently. Make sure the group realizes that the reason for looking at these models is to stimulate creative thinking about possibilities for

action that group members might like to be involved in or to initiate. In addition, the models provide hope, because they affirm that new action is possible.

Discuss the three questions given, or similar ones, after each model is presented. Then allow group members to share information they have gained about actions that are planned or being taken in your area.

Getting in Touch . . . : Use some of the opening paragraphs of this section to introduce your decision-making process.

Individual Work: Lead the group in a centering process and use 5 to 10 minutes for individuals to reflect on number 1 under Questions for Reflection.

Following this, ask group members to turn to "What Can You Do About It?" (page 42) to see if there are other actions they would like to consider. You may want to assign readings from the Resources in advance of this session.

Group Brainstorming: Encourage the group to share the possible actions they have thought of. Have two persons list them as they are called out, one to list individual actions and one to list corporate actions. As the group interacts, new ideas will come forth and participants will probably start building on one another's ideas. During this process, all ideas should be listed for all to see *without any evaluative comments*.

Decision Making: After the ideas cease to flow, allow time for each person to look back at their earlier work and to decide on some individual action that seems appropriate. If there is time, ask them to share their decision with one or two persons close by. Then move on to look at the suggested corporate actions. Although various persons may decide on particular corporate actions they would like to be part of or initiate with a different group, it may be that your group will want to initiate some action as a group. Ask for a show of hands to see how many women are initially interested in taking the different communal actions they have listed. Then, starting with the suggestion receiving the most votes, have the group discuss the following about each:

1. To what degree does this action move toward greater economic justice for women and consequently all human beings?
2. How much power do we as a group have to carry out or facilitate this action?

After discussion of the top-rated actions, try to help the group move toward consensus about which action(s) they as a group would like to undertake. All decisions do not have to be unanimous. It may be that five or six persons would like to work together on this or that action. If so, in the planning-for-action section, break the group into smaller units according to the action they have selected.

Planning for Action: You might have the following Action Plan Form duplicated for use during this final planning phase. At the top of an otherwise blank sheet list the following:

1. Step necessary to complete the action
2. Others (individuals or groups) we need to work with or contact
3. Persons responsible for action step or contact
4. Date begun
5. Date to be completed
6. Where the action will occur
7. Material needed
8. Cost

If you use the form, state that it is suggestive of the sorts of things that need to be thought through and the kinds of responsibility assignments that need to be made but need not be followed slavishly, and there may well be other aspects of planning that need to be done. According to the kinds of actions selected, you or smaller groups may need to schedule another meeting to complete the planning.

If the group did not decide on one or more actions to carry out as a whole, it would be extremely beneficial to schedule a sharing meeting for a later time when individuals and smaller groups could communicate the results or progress of their efforts. This might take place around a supper or social gathering. Certainly personal and group efforts will be strengthened by such sharing. The group may want to consider some form of staying in touch on an ongoing basis: for example, through continued meetings for study or action, a telephone network, or a newsletter. Don't be afraid to dream big and to expect that your group will want to undertake significant action for the transformation of our global village.

Close with prayer, providing time for individuals to share their concerns and hopes and using St. Francis's prayer in unison as a final petition by all.

RESOURCES

Justice for Women Working Groups

African Methodist Episcopal Church
Women's Missionary Society
2311 M Street NW
Washington, DC 20037

African Methodist Episcopal Zion Church
Woman's Home and Overseas Missionary Society
120 Nashville Boulevard
St. Albans, NY 11412

American Baptist Churches in the U.S.A.
Board of National Ministries
Valley Forge, PA 19481

Christian Church (Disciples of Christ)
222 South Downey Avenue
P.O. Box 1986
Indianapolis, IN 46206

Christian Methodist Episcopal Church
Woman's Missionary Council
P.O. Box 5245
Orlando, FL 32855

Church Women United in the U.S.A.
475 Riverside Drive, Room 812
New York, NY 10115

Episcopal Church Center
815 Second Avenue
New York, NY 10017

National Association of Ecumenical Staff
475 Riverside Drive, Room 870
New York, NY 10115

National Baptist Convention, U.S.A.
Woman's Auxiliary Convention
584 Arden Park
Detroit, MI 48202

National Council of the Churches of Christ
in the U.S.A.
Division of Church and Society
Justice for Women
475 Riverside Drive, Room 572
New York, NY 10115

National Council of Negro Women
of Greater New York
815 Second Avenue
New York, NY 10017

National Organization for Women
425 13th Street NW
Washington, DC 20004

Presbyterian Church (U.S.A.)
General Assembly Mission Board
Division of National Mission

Office of Women
341 Ponce de Leon Avenue NE
Atlanta, GA 30365

Presbyterian Church (U.S.A.)
Council on Women and the Church
475 Riverside Drive, Room 1151
New York, NY 10115

Presbyterian Church (U.S.A.)
Justice for Women
341 Ponce de Leon Avenue NE
Atlanta, GA 30365

Presbyterian Church (U.S.A.)
Office of Ministries with Racial and Ethnic Women
475 Riverside Drive, Room 1164
New York, NY 10115

Progressive National Baptist Convention
601 50th Street NE
Washington, DC 20019

Reformed Church in America
475 Riverside Drive, Room 1810
New York, NY 10115

United Church of Christ
United Church Board for Homeland Ministries
132 West 31st Street
New York, NY 10001

The United Methodist Church
General Board of Global Ministries
National Division
475 Riverside Drive, Room 338
New York, NY 10115

The United Methodist Church
General Board of Global Ministries
Women's Division
475 Riverside Drive, Room 1504
New York, NY 10115

YWCA of the U.S.A.
135 West 50th Street
New York, NY 10020

Organizations

A Woman's Yellow Pages. 570-plus organizations
concerned with women's issues.
Federation of Organizations for
Professional Women
2000 P Street NW
Washington, DC 20036

American Association of University Professors
Committee on the Status of Women
in the Academic Profession

One Dupont Circle, Suite 500
Washington, DC 20036

American Women's Clergy Association
The House of Imagene
214 P Street NW
Washington, DC 20001

Business and Professional Women's Foundation
2012 Massachusetts Avenue NW
Washington, DC 20036

Capitol Hill Women's Political Caucus
Room 1251 Dirksen Building
Washington, DC 20510

Coalition for a New Foreign and Military Policy
120 Maryland Avenue NE
Washington, DC 20002

Congressional Black Caucus
H 2344, Annex 2
Washington, DC 20515

Equity Policy Center
1302 18th Street NW
Washington, DC 20036

Homemakers Equal Rights Association
342 West Hornbeam Drive
Longwood, FL 32750

Human Rights for Women
1128 National Press Building
Washington, DC 20045

Interfaith Action for Economic Justice
110 Maryland Avenue NE
Washington, DC 20002

National Organization for Women
425 13th Street NW
Washington, DC 20004

Nuclear Weapons Freeze Campaign
National Clearinghouse
4144 Lindell Boulevard, Room 404
St. Louis, MO 63108

SANE: A Citizens' Organization for a Sane World
711 G Street SE
Washington, DC 20003

Third World Women's Project
Institute for Policy Studies
1901 Q Street NW
Washington, DC 20009

Women for Rural and Economic Equality
130 East 16th Street
New York, NY 10003

Women's International League for Peace and
  Freedom and Jane Addams Peace Association
1213 Race Street
Philadelphia, PA 19107

Women's International Resource
  Exchange Service
2700 Broadway, Room 7
New York, NY 10025

Women's Research and Education Institute
204 4th Street SE
Washington, DC 20003

Audiovisuals

Come a Long Way to Stand Here. Filmstrip/cassette with study guide, 60 minutes. For theological reflection and economic analysis, here is a series of four interviews with working women: Black, Hispanic, white, and Panamanian. Rental or purchase. Theology in the Americas, 475 Riverside Drive, Room 1258, New York, NY 10115.

Controlling Interest: The World of the Multinational Corporation. Color film, 16mm., 40 minutes. This documentary focuses on the impact of policies and actions of large international corporations as they affect Third World nations and U.S. workers. Rental. EcuFilm, 810 Twelfth Avenue South, Nashville, TN 37203.

Forget Not Our Sisters: Women Under Apartheid. Slide show and cassette. Rental. Boston CSLA, P.O. Box 879, Boston, MA 02114.

Glass House. Color film, 16mm., 12 minutes, Teleketics (Franciscan Communications Center, 1229 South Santee Street, Los Angeles, CA 90015). This is an allegorical film about a wealthy man and "his" maid who are surrounded by working peasants, making a point about the destructive nature of unrestrained and unshared affluence. Rental. Materials Distribution Service, 341 Ponce de Leon Avenue NE, Atlanta, GA 30365; also available from EcuFilm.

Growing Up Under the Nuclear Shadow. Color film, 16mm., 26 minutes. In this documentary film, young people speak about their fears of nuclear war and call for an end to the arms race. Rental. EcuFilm, 810 Twelfth Avenue South, Nashville, TN 37203.

Guess Who's Coming to Breakfast. Color filmstrip, cassette tape, script, and guide, 19 minutes. This filmstrip shows the impact of one multinational corporation on the economy and life-style of people in the Caribbean nation of Santo Domingo. Purchase. Packard Manse Media Project, 583 Plain Street, Stoughton, MA 02072.

I Have a Nuclear War Inside Me. Film, 16mm. Elementary and high school students meet in their classrooms with Roberta Snow and Eric Chivian of Educators for Social Responsibility to share their thoughts and fears. Educators for Social Responsibility, 639 Massachusetts Avenue, Cambridge, MA 02139.

I Have Three Children. Slide show and cassette, 20 minutes. A powerful antinuclear documentary, narrated by Dr. Helen Caldicott. Rental. Women's International League for Peace and Freedom, 1213 Race Street, Philadelphia, PA 19107.

Institutional Violence. Slide show and cassette. Part I, 90 frames, 18 minutes, looks at racism, sexism, militarism, and economic exploitation; Part II, 60 frames, 12 minutes, takes a deeper look at economic exploitation. Rental. The Institute for Peace and Justice, 4144 Lendell, Room 400, St. Louis, MO 63108.

Killing Us Softly: Advertising's Image of Women. Color film, 16mm., 30 minutes. This film examines advertising as a means of selling not just products but values, goals, and attitudes toward love and sexuality. Rental. Cambridge Documentary Films, Inc., P.O. Box 385, Cambridge, MA 02139.

The Last Epidemic. Color film, 16mm., 35 minutes. This jolting documentary summarizes the Physicians for Social Responsibility symposium in 1980. Physicians or Social Responsibility, 639 Massachusetts Avenue, Cambridge, MA 02139.

The Life and Times of Rosie the Riveter. Film, 16mm., 60 minutes. A heartwarming documentary about women who worked in factories at the beginning of World War II, only to be told to leave when the war ended. Mixing period newsreels with interviews of the women makes an entertainingly relevant film. Clarity Educational Films, P.O. Box 315, Franklin Lakes, NJ 07417.

Malnutrition, the Hidden Killer. Film, 16mm., 23 minutes. This provides an overview of world hunger, poverty, and development and their relationships. Borrow from Church World Service Film Library, 28606 Phillips Street, Elkhart, IN 46515.

A Matter of Sex. Film, shown on NBC-TV network, January 16, 1984. This describes the Willmar 8 women organizing in a bank. Cultural Information Service, P.O. Box 786, Madison Square Station, New York, NY 10159.

No Frames, No Boundaries. Film, 16mm., 28 minutes. The "bad news" of the nuclear arms race is set in the context of the "good news" of global physical and spiritual unity. There are striking views of earth from space. Creative Initiative, 222 High Street, Palo Alto, CA 94301.

Poverty Has a Woman's Face. Video tape, 20 minutes. An examination of the feminization of poverty prepared in North Carolina for the Governor's Conference on Women and the Economy by WTVD-TV. North Carolina Council on the Status of Women, 526 North Wilmington Street, Raleigh, NC 27604.

The Race That Nobody Wins. Slide show and tape, 20 minutes. This detailed account of the stockpiling of arms and the monetary and social cost of this stockpiling describes economic conversion legislation that could slow down and ultimately stop the arms race. Rental. The Institute for Peace and Justice, 4144 Lindell, Room 400, St. Louis, MO 63108.

Sharing Global Resources. Slide show and tape, 45 minutes. The presentation explores the need for a new international economic order and new internal economic arrangements in First and Third World countries. Rental. Women's International League for Peace and Freedom, 1213 Race Street, Philadelphia, PA 19107.

War Without Winners. Film, 16mm., 28 minutes. This good and fresh appeal to reason, directed by Haskell Wexler for the Center for Defense Information, presents both military experts and ordinary people of the U.S. and the U.S.S.R. expressing their fears, thoughts, and hopes about the future, with the grim possibility of the incineration of civilization in minutes. Films, Inc., 733 Green Bay Road, Wilmette, IL 60091.

Willmar 8. Color film and study guide, 16mm., 55 minutes. A tense documentary in which eight women are pitted against the ostracism and silence of an entire community because of their two-year fight for equal pay by their employer, a local Minnesota bank. Rental. EcuFilm, 810 Twelfth Avenue South, Nashville, TN 37203.

Where to Obtain Legislative Information

Too often world legislation and public policy can prove intimidating for women. Yet when Congress is in session, numerous bills that have a direct and indirect effect on the economic status of women are introduced. Although women constitute more than 50 percent of the population, there are all too few representatives of women in Congress. Thus there is a necessity for women both to increase their awareness of legislative initiatives impacting their lives and the lives of other women, at home and abroad, and to become more involved in making their voices heard within the legislative branch.

For information about proposed legislation affecting women nationally and internationally, contact:

Congressional Caucus for Women's Issues
2471 Rayburn Building
Washington, DC 20515
(202) 225-6740
or
Women's Equity Action League
805 15th Street NW, Suite 822
Washington, DC 20005
(202) 638-1961

The following are available from WEAL at the above address:

WEAL Washington Report. Focuses on issues of concern to women: current legislation, Supreme

Court rulings, Executive Branch action.

WEAL's Economic Agenda for Women (1983). A summary of major legal and economic issues, with statistics and recommendations for reform.

To contact your elected officials in Washington, the addresses are:

President _____
The White House
1600 Pennsylvania Avenue NW
Washington, DC 20500
(202) 456-7639

The Honorable _____
U.S. Senate
Washington, DC 20510
(202) 224-3121

The Honorable _____
U.S. House of Representatives
Washington, DC 20515
(202) 224-3121

Further Reading

Books and Magazine Articles

Abrecht, Paul, and Koshy Ninan, eds. *Before It's Too Late: The Challenge of Nuclear Disarmament.* World Council of Churches, 1983.

Adams, Ruth, and Susan Cullen, eds. *The Final Epidemic: Physicians and Scientists on Nuclear War.* Educational Foundation for Nuclear Science, 1981.

Alter, JoAnne. *A Part-Time Career for a Full-Time You.* Houghton Mifflin Co., 1982.

Anderson, Lucy. "Work." Ch. 7 in *Taking Charge: Achieving Personal and Political Change Through Simple Living.* Simple Living Collective. Bantam Books, 1977.

Barnet, Richard. *The Roots of War.* Penguin Books, 1973.

Bell, Carolyn Shaw. "Women at Work: An Economic Appraisal." In Ann Stromberg and Shirley Harkess, eds., *Women Working: Theories and Facts in Perspective.* Mayfield Publishing Co., 1978.

Benson, Bernard. *The Peace Book.* Bantam Books, 1982.

Birch, Bruce C., and Larry L. Rasmussen. *The Predicament of the Prosperous.* Westminster Press, 1978.

Brown, Peter G., and Henry Shue, eds. *The Border That Joins: Mexican Migrants and U.S. Responsibility.* Rowman & Littlefield, 1983.

Brown, Robert McAfee. *Making Peace in the Global Village.* Westminster Press, 1981.

Brown, Sydney. "New Styles of Work." In Dieter T. Hessel, ed., *Congregational Lifestyle Change for the Lean Years.* Program Agency, The United Presbyterian Church U.S.A., 1981.

Chapman, Jane Roberts, ed. *Economic Independence for Women: The Foundation for Equal Rights.* Sage Publications, 1976.

Christ, Carol P., and Judith Plaskow, eds. *Womanspirit Rising: A Feminist Reader in Religion.* Harper & Row, 1979.

Clark, Linda, et al. *Image-Breaking/Image-Building.* Pilgrim Press, 1981.

Cochran, Thomas B., et al. *Nuclear Weapons Databook.* Vols. 1 and 2. Ballinger Publishing Co., 1983.

Collins, Sheila D. *A Different Heaven and Earth.* Judson Press, 1974.

Creating Our Future. Educators for Social Responsibility (639 Massachusetts Avenue, Cambridge, MA 02139), 1982.

Ehrenreich, Barbara, and Karin Stallard. "The Nouveau Poor." *Ms.,* July/August 1982.

Feinstein, Karen Wolk, ed. *Working Women and Families.* Sage Publications, 1979.

Fiorenza, Elisabeth Schüssler. *In Memory of Her: A Feminist Theological Reconstruction of Early Christian Beginnings.* Crossroad Publishing Co., 1983.

Forisha, Barbara L., and Barbara H. Goldman, eds. *Outsiders on the Inside: Women and Organizations.* Prentice-Hall (Spectrum Book), 1981.

George, Susan. *How the Other Half Dies: The Real Reasons for World Hunger.* Allanheld, Osmun & Co., 1977.

Gilligan, Carol. *In a Different Voice: Psychological Theory and Women's Development.* Harvard University Press, 1982.

Goldfarb, Ronald L. *Migrant Farm Workers: A Caste of Despair.* Iowa State University Press, 1981.

Grannis, J. Christopher, et al. *The Risk of the Cross: Christian Discipleship in the Nuclear Age.* Seabury Press, 1981.

Gray, Elizabeth Dodson. *Green Paradise Lost: Re-Mything Genesis.* Roundtable Press, 1979.

Grune, Joy Ann, ed. *Manual on Pay Equity: Raising Wages for Women's Work.* Conference on Alternative State and Local Policies, May 1980. Committee on Pay Equity, 2000 Florida Avenue NW, Room 400W, Washington, DC 20009.

Gutiérrez, Gustavo, and Richard Shaull. *Liberation and Change.* John Knox Press, 1977.

Howe, Florence, ed. *Women and the Power to Change.* McGraw-Hill Book Co., 1975.

Huston, Perdita. *Third World Women Speak Out: Interviews in Six Countries on Change, Development, and Basic Needs.* Praeger Publishers, 1979.

Kennard, Byron. *Nothing Can Be Done, Everything Is Possible.* Brick House Publishing Co., 1982.

Keyes, Ken, Jr. *The Hundredth Monkey.* Vision Books, 1981.

Kraybill, Donald B. *Facing Nuclear War: A Plea for*

Christian Witness. Herald Press, 1982.

Kreps, Juanita M., ed. *Women and the American Economy: A Look to the 1980s.* Prentice-Hall, 1980.

LaRouche, Janice, and Regina Ryan. *Janice LaRouche's Strategies for Women and Work.* Avon Books, 1984.

Lewis, Sasha G. *Slave Trade Today: American Exploitation of Illegal Aliens.* Beacon Press, 1979.

Lindsay, Beverly, ed. *Comparative Perspectives of Third World Women: The Impact of Race, Sex, and Class.* Praeger Publishers, 1980.

Long, Edward LeRoy, Jr. *Peace Thinking in a Warring World.* Westminster Press, 1983.

Macy, Joanna Rogers. *Despair and Personal Power in the Nuclear Age.* New Society Publishers, 1983.

Nash, June, and Marie-Patricia Fernandez-Kelly, eds. *Women, Men, and the International Division of Labor.* State University of New York Press, 1983.

Olmstead, Barney, and Suzanne Smith. *The Job-Sharing Handbook.* Penguin Books, 1983.

Papa, Mary Bader. *Christian Feminism: Completing the Subtotal Woman.* Fides/Caretian, 1981.

Pasquariello, Ronald D. *Faith, Justice, and Our Nation's Budget: An Action Guide for Christian Citizens.* Judson Press, 1982.

Piven, Frances Fox. "Women and the State: Ideology, Power, and the Welfare State." *Socialist Review,* March/April 1984.

Rasmussen, Larry L. *Economic Anxiety and Christian Faith.* Augsburg Publishing House, 1981.

Richardson, John M., Jr., ed. *Making It Happen: A Positive Guide to the Future.* U.S. Association for the Club of Rome, 1982.

Ross, Stanley R., ed. *Views Across the Border: The United States and Mexico.* University of New Mexico Press, 1978.

Ruether, Rosemary Radford. *New Woman, New Earth: Sexist Ideologies and Human Liberation.* Seabury Press, 1975.

————. *The Radical Kingdom: The Western Experience of Messianic Hope.* Paulist Press, 1975.

————. *Sexism and God Talk: Toward a Feminist Theology.* Beacon Press, 1983.

Seller, Maxine Schwartz, ed. *Immigrant Women.* Temple University Press, 1981.

Smith, Jackie M. *Partners in Pluralism.* Friendship Press, 1981.

Strharsky, Harry, ed. *Must We Choose Sides?* Christian Commitment for the '80s: vol. 1. Inter-Religious Task Force for Social Analysis, 1979.

———— and Mary L. Suhor, eds. *Which Side Are We On?* Christian Commitment for the '80s: vol. 2. Inter-Religious Task Force for Social Analysis, 1980.

Suarez, Cecilia Cota-Robles, and Lupe Anguiano. *Every Woman's Right: The Right to Quality Education and Economic Independence.* Education Development Center/WEEA Publishing Center (55 Chapel Street, Suite 201, Newton, MA 02160).

Terkel, Studs. *American Dreams: Lost and Found.* Pantheon Books, 1980.

————. *Working.* Pantheon Books, 1974.

Van Vuuren, Nancy. *Work and Career.* Choices: Guides for Today's Woman. Westminster Press, 1983.

Verdesi, Elizabeth Howell. *In But Still Out: Women in the Church.* Westminster Press, 1976.

Other Printed Material

Human Needs: Unfinished Business on the Nation's Agenda. League of Women Voters Education Fund, 1730 M Street NW, Washington, DC 20036.

Inequality of Sacrifice: The Impact of the Reagan Budget on Women. Coalition on Women and the Budget, 1984. National Women's Law Center, 1751 N Street NW, Washington, DC 20036.

International Feminism: Networking Against Female Sexual Slavery. International Women's Tribune Centre (IWTC), 305 E. 46th Street, 6th Floor, New York, NY 10017.

Last Hired, First Fired: Layoffs and Civil Rights. Washington, DC: Government Printing Office, 1977.

Legislation and Women Fact Sheets, including Affirmative Action, Comparable Worth, Human Life Amendment/Bill, Title IX, and Women Growing Older Fact Sheet (1983); *Sex Discrimination in Insurance: A Guide for Women; Social Security and Women* (1983). Women's Equity Action League, 805 15th Street NW, Suite 822, Washington, DC 20005.

Poverty in the American Dream: Women and Children First, by Karin Stallard, Barbara Ehrenreich, and Holly Sklar. Institute for New Communications (INC), 853 Broadway, Room 905, New York, NY 10003.

The Transnational Economy. The Institute for Policy Studies. 1901 Q Street NW, Washington, DC 20009.

U.S. Department of Labor Packet. Material on statistical information related to women's issues. U.S. Department of Labor, Office of the Secretary, Women's Bureau, Washington, DC 20210.

What About the Children: The Threat of Nuclear War and Our Responsibility to Preserve This Planet for Future Generations. Parents and Teachers for Social Responsibility, P.O. Box 517, Moretown, VT 05660.

Women and Economic Justice: Give Us This Day Our Daily Bread. Council on Women and the Church, 475 Riverside Drive, Room 1151, New York, NY 10115.

Women and the Economy Packet. Includes "Our Nation and the Profit System" and "Does Women's Work Count?" by D. Steffens. Women's International League for Peace and Freedom, 1213 Race Street, Philadelphia, PA 19107.

Women in the Global Factory. Pamphlet no. 2 by Annette Fuentes and Barbara Ehrenreich. Institute for New Communications, 853 Broadway, Room 905, New York, NY 10003.

"Women, Men, and the Division of Labor," by Kathleen Newland, *Worldwatch,* Paper 37, May 1980.

Women and Poverty: A Research Summary by Mary Rubin. Business and Professional Women's Foundation, 2012 Massachusetts Avenue NW, Washington, DC 20036.

"Working Women: A Handbook of Resources, Rights, and Remedies," in *Southern Exposure,* Winter 1981, edited by Tobi Lippin. Southern Exposure, P.O. Box 531, Durham, NC 27702.